Persuasive Writing

Books that make you better

Books that make you better. That make you *be* better, *do* better, *feel* better. Whether you want to upgrade your personal skills or change your job, whether you want to improve your managerial style, become a more powerful communicator, or be stimulated and inspired as you work.

Prentice Hall Business is leading the field with a new breed of skills, careers and development books. Books that are a cut above the mainstream – in topic, content and delivery – with an edge and verve that will make you better, with less effort.

Books that are as sharp and smart as you are.

Prentice Hall Business.
We work harder – so you don't have to.

For more details on products, and to contact us, visit
www.pearsoned.co.uk

Persuasive Writing

How to harness the power of words

Peter Frederick

Prentice Hall
is an imprint of

Harlow, England • London • New York • Boston • San Francisco • Toronto • Sydney • Singapore • Hong Kong
Tokyo • Seoul • Taipei • New Delhi • Cape Town • Madrid • Mexico City • Amsterdam • Munich • Paris • Milan

Pearson Education Limited

Edinburgh Gate
Harlow CM20 2JE
Tel: +44 (0)1279 623623
Fax: +44 (0)1279 431059
Website: www.pearsoned.co.uk

First published in Great Britain in 2011

Pearson Education is not responsible for the content of third party internet sites.

ISBN: 978-0-273-74613-3

British Library Cataloguing-in-Publication Data
A catalogue record for this book is available from the British Library

Library of Congress Cataloging-in-Publication Data
Frederick, Peter.
   Persuasive writing : how to harness the power of words / Peter Frederick.
      p. cm.
   Includes index.
   ISBN 978-0-273-74613-3 (pbk.)
   1. Business writing.   2. Report writing.   3. Persuasion (Rhetoric)   I. Title.
   HF5718.3.F74 2001
   808'.06665--dc22

10 9 8 7 6 5 4 3 2 1
15 14 13 12 11

Typeset in 10pt Iowan Old Style BT by 3
Printed and bound in Great Britain by Henry Ling Ltd, Dorchester, Dorset

Contents

About the author

PETER FREDERICK has spent the last ten years persuading people with money to hand it over. More specifically, as the Senior Bid Consultant at Pera Innovation, he persuades national and European bodies to fund innovative research on behalf of Pera's clients. Peter supports bid writers through every step of the process, from concept review through to final submission, to ensure their proposals have the best possible chance of success. It seems to be working: in the last three years his expertise has been used to secure projects worth over £200 million. Beyond Pera, Peter's training, writing guidelines and evaluation skills are used by a network of research centres across Europe, including the likes of QinetiQ and Fraunhofer Institute. Peter's expertise is not only restricted to research funding; he also works on corporate communications, sales collateral and, most recently, commercial and charity bids. And, as you may have noticed, he's started writing books.

Introduction

If you write something for someone else to read, the chances are you are doing it to get a result. In other words, you want to persuade the reader to do what you want. This applies equally to a range of documents, such as emails, CVs, reports, advertising and recruitment ads.

Most of my time is spent training writers how to win funding for industrial research. This intensely competitive process gives you one shot at winning a grant, with no right to reply. I have spent the last ten years developing practical persuasive techniques, proving them on multi-million-pound grant applications and teaching them to bid writers across Europe. More recently, I've successfully applied these techniques to other areas of life and business, such as CVs, business reviews, sales documents and charity bids.

This book began as a more useful alternative to course notes (you know, like the pile of slide printouts you have tucked away in a drawer somewhere, never to be read again). As such, it doesn't include lots of musings, anecdotes or long-winded analogies. Instead it concentrates on the practical application of persuasive writing techniques, illustrated with real-world examples.

Persuasive writing is the art of understanding what you want, why someone else would give it to you and then asking them in the most efficient and effective way. This book brings together the most useful insights from concise writing techniques and decision theory to help you do just that. You will learn how to:

■ Understand why you are writing, who you are writing for and what response you need from them to get what you want.

- Use reason, logic and emotion to persuade your reader and learn how to tell stories to your audience, even in business documents.

- Understand why we make illogical decisions and how to use these errors of reasoning to your best advantage.

- Cut the fat from your writing and create punchy, effective text by using a proven seven-step process.

- Use verbs to give energy to your writing.

- Avoid common mistakes including spelling, punctuation and poor word choice.

- Plan and structure your writing to simplify the writing process and increase readability.

- Improve the look and feel of your document through font choice, bullets, headings and graphics.

- Master common document types including emails, web pages, CVs and grant bids.

- Master the dark arts of persuasion to manipulate your reader and secure your aims when all else fails.

Whether it's for business or pleasure; whether you're writing the longest report or the shortest email; if you write anything hoping to get a result, this book is for you.

Acknowledgements

We are grateful to the following for permission to reproduce copyright material:

Image on p.100 courtesy of AFP/ Getty Images; figures on pages 122–3 courtesy of Pera Innovation Ltd.

In some instances we have been unable to trace the owners of copyright material, and we would appreciate any information that would enable us to do so.

1

What is Persuasive Writing?

Persuasive writing is any writing that aims to get a result. In business, this is everything you write. If you are not trying to get a result, why are you writing?

Examples include:

- a cover letter for a job application;
- an email letting staff know about a new policy;
- a competitive tender;
- a letter seeking to recover a bad debt.

All of these require some sort of response from the reader; hence they need to be *persuasive*. Even fiction writing needs to be persuasive. The author must convince an audience that the fiction is real. If there is no suspension of disbelief, the author has failed.

In short, persuasive writing is everything you will ever write to be read by another person.[1]

This section helps you ask the key questions:

1 Why are you writing?

2 Who will be reading?

3 What's your intended result?

4 What response do you need from your audience to get that result?

---

1 OK, there are some exceptions (such as transcription) but it's not a bad assumption to make.

WHY ARE YOU WRITING?

Is writing the best medium?

It has been said that only 7 per cent of face-to-face communication is verbal. Whilst this is almost certainly not true except in very specific circumstances,[2] face-to-face communication does have many advantages. When writing, you do not have access to the persuasive tools of face-to-face contact. You can't roll your eyes, express sarcasm, gesture or look trustworthy. If you have charm and charisma, persuading in person can be easier and more effective.

However, writing has many advantages face-to-face contact doesn't: you have time to craft your words; you can edit and seek opinion; you can write in your pyjamas, eat as much garlic as you like and you don't have to wash.

Writing is slow, considered and precise, where personal contact is fast, dynamic and free-form. Think carefully and, where you have a choice, choose the medium most likely to persuade.

Objectives

As already mentioned, persuasive writing should yield a result. As such, you need to define that intended result before you start writing.

Using the examples on the previous page, the intended results might be:

■ an invitation to interview;

---

2   The research from which this claim is derived focused only on communicating feelings and attitudes, not communication in general.

- 90% of staff implementing the new policy within seven days;
- winning the competitive tender;
- the bad debt being paid in full within 28 days.

Although setting objectives may sound fairly obvious, there are still a number of common pitfalls:

1 too many objectives;

2 losing sight of the objective;

3 not answering the question.

Too many objectives

"I want to let the staff know about the pay freeze. And the office refurbishment. And the new director. And boost morale. And make profits shoot up 20%."

OK, so the last bit is a slight exaggeration but you get the point. We are often tempted to include every bit of news we have in one communication. This is especially true for sending bulk emails. However, remember that most people will only absorb one message from any one communication, so make sure that is all you give them.

You may have some sub-objectives, but make sure they are realistic. For example:

"Let staff know about the pay freeze and keep angry replies to less than 5% of staff."

This is probably fine, and the objective of minimising angry replies will encourage you to word your message sensitively. However:

"Let staff know about the pay freeze and raise morale"

is probably asking a bit much.

Even in longer documents, such as annual reports or sales proposals, there should still be a single aim, even if you have sub-objectives beneath this.

Losing sight of the objective

We've all been there. We write a lengthy document or email that we think is going to knock the socks off any reader, and then find no one has a clue what we were on about. We have lost sight of our objectives.

Letters of complaint are a perfect example. Why are you complaining? What do you want to happen? If you are after a refund, this should be the focus of every letter you send to the company, not just the first. It is very easy to get side-tracked by numbers and dates and who to blame, and forget the point of writing in the first place. That said, if your objective is to have a good rant, carry on.

Not answering the question

In business, much of what we write is in response to a question or request. This applies equally to intra-office emails and competitive tenders. The person you are replying to is expecting a specific result. If they have clearly asked for that result, make sure they get it. Likewise, if you claim you are going to show something, make sure you actually show it.

Here's an example from a competitive tender (complete with original spelling):

2.2.7 – Efficient facilitation of tasks through direct availability of key equipment

Since Project x's development is highly dependant of specialized equipment, the main partners will be responsible for providing them. The division of work for each company within the consortium makes them the sole responsible for acquiring/hiring the necessary apparatus for completing their tasks.

First of all, this is a horrible piece of disjointed writing. Even worse, the writer has introduced the paragraph with a very definite heading, and then failed completely to provide the evidence to support that heading. The writer needed to show that key equipment is available but has ended up showing that each partner is responsible for acquiring equipment, not the same thing at all.

Again, this may all sound very simple but it is the simple things that tend to be forgotten when you are in a hurry.

WHO IS YOUR AUDIENCE?

"Johnny isn't feeling very well. He has a poorly tummy. Poor Johnny. Johnny won't be able to chair the remuneration committee today."

If this were aimed at a four-year-old (with a good understanding of remuneration committees), it would be fine. However, it's not so good if you are apologising to the board for missing work. If you do not understand what your audience expects, you will never be persuasive.

Some things to remember about your audience

Regardless of who your audience is, they will have certain things in common. The following six are fairly safe bets:

- **Your audience is an ignorant genius.** Assume your reader is at least as intelligent as you but has no knowledge of the subject, unless you are absolutely certain they do. This will help keep jargon to a minimum and help you avoid patronising your audience.

- **Your audience has an inner cynic.** Whenever we read, we have a cynical voice inside our heads, questioning each phrase. Make sure you keep that little voice quiet by telling your audience what you really mean in a clear and believable fashion. Using rhetorical questions[3] is useful here. Effectively, you are asking the questions their little voice will ask, and then answering them immediately. This allows the audience to relate to you, and builds trust and empathy.

- **Your audience creates the meaning.** Words are just squiggles on a piece of paper, until interpreted. People will interpret your words through their own experiences and biases (see Chapter 3) and hence may understand something in a completely different manner than you intended. This is why two people can use the same document to argue completely opposite views and each believes the document supports their own particular view.

- **Your audience has better things to do**. Amazing but true. Quite frankly, stapling my tongue to the table is more appealing than reading some documents. If you want your audience to read your work, make it rewarding, entertaining and engaging for them.

- **Your audience will skim-read.** This is a direct result of having better things to do. Make the information as accessible as possible. In fact, if you are reading this bit, I'd be surprised.

- **Your audience wants to be hooked**. Once a reader has made an investment in reading your text, they want confirmation it was a sound investment. Losing them early on will make them angry with you and themselves. The longer you keep them hooked, the more they will give you the benefit of the doubt (see Chapter 3 for why this happens).

---

3 Questions that you do not expect the audience to answer.

All of these points require you to understand who you are writing for. Sometimes, you won't know your audience. If this is the case, make some assumptions and build up a typical audience model. It may help to create a 'best-case' reader and a 'worst-case' reader to make sure you are not alienating any one group.

In assessing your audience, consider:

- name (if known)
- gender
- age
- level of education
- occupation
- relationship to you
- reasons for reading
- where they are likely to read
- when they are likely to read
- hostility/cynicism rating.[4]

Once you have your reader in mind, consider what this means for your writing.

If they are busy or very cynical, don't dress up what you have to say in lots of excess text. If your audience is a lexiophile (look it up), supply a veritable smorgasbord of stimulating sentences. Don't forget why you are writing though: you need to understand your audience in order to persuade them effectively.

---

4 How hostile is the reader to you? This is an important factor for managers to remember when writing to their staff.

Persuade your audience, not yourself

You have taken a sales job in a BMW car showroom. You have fallen in love with a jet black Z4 coupé, an expensive two-seater sports car. Whilst this may indeed be the best car in the show-room, you would quickly be out of a job if this were the only car you ever tried to sell. Customers come in with different requirements and, as a salesman, you change what you offer accordingly. Exactly the same thing applies to writing: make sure the text you offer to the reader is tailored to their needs and is not simply what you consider to be exceptional writing.

The world of advertising is littered with the remains of cam-paigns written for an audience of one. Websites also provide plenty of examples. The text below is from a typical consultant's website:

Productizing information assets

Leverage cross-enterprise knowledge investments

Survival in a fast-moving corporate world depends on rapid repur-posing in response to environmental change by productizing untapped information assets held by disparate stakeholders across multiple platforms. Acecorp Consulting are world leaders in identifying and leveraging knowledge investments through our synergistic turnkey interventions.

If you are an IT consultant, this sounds great. Unfortunately, this company's customers are not IT consultants. The only reason I read beyond the title was because I had to. I think the paragraph is trying to say this:

Making money from your information

Exploit your cross-company knowledge

Your business depends on your ability to respond to change. By bringing together and exploiting knowledge held across your organisation, you can respond faster. Acecorp Consulting are world leaders in informa-tion management and our easy-to-use collaborative solutions will help you identify and exploit your corporate knowledge.

Remember: persuade your audience, not yourself.

Adapt your style – moving from academic to business writing

In the UK, around half of all people writing at work will have been to university. Academia teaches a particular writing style, ideally suited to presenting research. However, some of the traits that make this style so good at its job can hamper it when applied to business writing:

Careful language

An academic paper must be absolutely sure before it can defini-tively state something is true. As a result, the language tends to be very non-committal (*"this seems to indicate"* rather than *"this shows"*). The author will also include lots of background detail, caveats and references to avoid any misunderstanding. In busi-ness writing, being this cautious in your language can sometimes weaken your message's impact. For example, in advertising, you wouldn't have a price comparison website saying:

> *"Some people, with particular driving histories, may be able to reduce their annual vehicle insurance costs, depending on their current insur-ance provider and exact insurance requirements. However, further study is required to ascertain if savings on initial insurance payments translate into an improved financial situation long term."*

Unless you are absolutely sure you can't be, try to be definite and positive with your writing. Where you do need to include caveats, don't over-emphasise them; persuade the reader first, then feed in the caveats.

Writing in the third person

This is very clinical and detached, but lacks warmth. Writing in the first person is warmer, friendlier and allows you to talk about the reader more easily.

Supersized words

A typical academic paper tends to match the complexity of its general words to the complexity of the jargon (subject-specific words). As discussed in Chapter 5, cutting out the supersized words really improves clarity and helps your message come across.

Of course, if you are writing for an audience of academics, you will be more persuasive writing in a more academic style. The key is to adapt your style to persuade your audience.

READER RESPONSE = RESULT

We know our audience. We know our objective. Now for the tricky part: how do we persuade our audience to help us achieve our objective? This all comes down to reader response.

Reader response is made up of two parts:

Emotional response. This is the feeling created inside the reader (pity, sadness, elation, etc).

Intent response. This is what the reader intends to do as a result of these feelings (buy something, stop doing something, etc).

Take the example of a competitive tender. A good bid will have all the required content. A great bid will also elicit an emotional response from the assessor that increases the odds of the assessor favouring that bid.

The ultimate aim for a persuasive writer is to elicit responses such as:

"That's terrible, I must do something to help."

"This is clearly urgent, I'll get it done straight away."

"That's really clever, I like that advert."

The last one of these does not directly lead to an intent response but the intended result may be to build brand identity rather than persuade people to buy the product. The drinks brand Guinness has famously used this technique in their 'Believe', 'Dancing Man' and 'Evolution' adverts. These ads weren't created by accident. The advertisers had a clear objective to build brand awareness, they understood what would appeal to their audience and created the correct response (happiness at being entertained, intellectual stimulation) to achieve their intended result.

Different responses for different readers

What is your aim in creating a job advert? You may create it to attract a particular type of candidate. In addition, you will almost certainly want to discourage unsuitable candidates from applying, or you will be overrun with applications.

Job adverts will use phrases such as "you must have at least a master's degree". This attracts qualified candidates, who feel a sense of achievement in meeting your high standards. In addition, it puts off unqualified candidates. Similarly, deliberately using very simple or very complex language helps you attract the right audience at the same time as discouraging the wrong one.

So, make sure you think about creating positive and negative reader responses depending on who you want to get a result from.

Calls to action and reader rewards

As a general rule of persuasive writing, tell your reader how to do what you want them to do. Try not to order your reader to do something; it should be their decision. However, once they've made this decision, you should give them all the tools they need to act on it. This is sometimes termed the 'Call to action'. Without it, you run the risk of your reader agreeing with you but doing nothing about it.

Rule 1: include a call to action in your document

A call to action is made up of two parts:

1 Here's what you can do.

2 Here's how you can do it.

The first builds on the intent response. The reader wants to do something about the situation but may not necessarily know what to do (or what you want them to do), so make it clear. The second element then provides the tools. This is the where, who, when and how of the solution.

Examples of calls to action could be:

> *"Please call me on 01234 567890 before 10:00 to let me know your decision."*

> *"To take advantage of this offer, email sales@acecorp.com."*

If you have the luxury of time,[5] you may look to involve your reader more in the process of being persuaded. Reader participation is best when they get something out of it. This is

---

5 E.g. advertising, where the reader response does not have to be instantaneous.

a fundamental lesson for fiction writers but it also applies to business writing.

Consider a request to your boss to solve a problem. You may know the solution and could easily ask them[6] to implement it. However, you may get a better response by presenting the problem and leading them to the point of the solution without actually stating it. This gives your boss a chance to participate by solving the problem for you. Your boss has been rewarded through some mental stimulation and is likely to be happier implementing the solution, thus achieving your result. Most importantly, it will be their idea and this will strongly influence its chance of happening, as explained in Chapter 3. Clearly, this requires knowledge of your audience to know if this will work.

SUMMARY

Persuasive writing is every document you will ever write to be read by another person. Before you start, ask yourself the following:

- **Why are you writing?**
  - Is there a better option?
  - Does your document actually do what you are setting out to do?
- **Who are you writing for?**
  - Do I really know them?
  - Am I trying to persuade them or myself?

---

6 Bizarrely, there is no official gender-neutral way of referring to a single person in English. I could use 'he' in all cases and be accused of sexism or use 'they' and upset the grammar purists. As there isn't a paramilitary wing of the *Oxford English Dictionary*, I'm using 'them' in this book.

When planning what to write, remember **Reader Response** equals **Result**:

- know what you want (**Result**),
- who you want it from (**Reader**) and
- the **Response** most likely to lead to that result.

To make sure you get the result you want, make sure you include a **call to action** to let the reader know exactly what they should do next.

2

Tools for Persuasive Writing

The first chapter of this book emphasised how important it is to be persuasive and gave you the basic mantra of persuasive writing. This chapter builds on this by giving you some more tools to use in your writing to generate the correct reader response.

This section will cover the following:

- Ethos, Logos, Pathos
- Using emotive language
- You, We, I
- FABU
- Storytelling:
    - the seven basic plots
    - the seven basic needs
- A persuasive writing example.

ETHOS, LOGOS, PATHOS

Despite first impressions, these aren't anything to do with musketeers. In fact, these are Aristotle's[1] three modes of persuasion. They break down as follows:

Ethos

This refers to moral competence, expertise and knowledge. In order to be persuasive, an audience must believe that the speaker is someone to whom they want to listen. This can also be termed 'respect'. Respect is specific to the audience. If you are a leading expert in the use of Intensity-Modulated Radiation

---

1   A Greek philosopher in the 4th century BC. A student of Plato, Aristotle was a biologist, physicist, poet, ethicist and all-round clever chap.

Therapy (IMRT) for cancer treatment, you will be respected when you speak on that subject. If you try to use that expertise to get a street gang to respect you, you will most likely fail.

In writing, you should use your reputation to earn respect. If you have no reputation with your audience, build it through the quality of your writing. If you are succinct, accurate and persuasive, your audience is more likely to respect you and thus respond to your writing.

Logos

Logos is the root of the word 'logic'. Readers will always respond best to an argument that has a logical element to it. The word of power here is 'because'. If readers are given a reason, they are more likely to respond in the way you want them to.

Pathos

The last of the three, pathos, refers to emotions. If you play with the readers' emotions, you can get some very powerful results. We'll discuss this more below.

You may recall the mnemonic Reader Response = Result. This can be extended using our three principles above to make:

Reason, Respect and Emotion[2] = Reader Response = Result

In Appendix 4 you will find a flow diagram illustrating how all these aspects of persuasion come together. For now, however, just remember your three musketeers and you'll be fine.

---

2 If anyone can come up with a synonym for 'emotion' beginning with 'R', I'd like to know ...

USING EMOTIVE LANGUAGE

If you are an engineer or a scientist, you're probably cowering under the desk at the moment. Despite the years of training engineers have received telling them to avoid emotion in writing, persuasive writing relies on it. Remember our motto:

Reader Response = Result.

The reader response depends on how well you can manipulate their emotions. This doesn't mean being theatrical:

> *"Please, I'm begging you, my children will starve to death if you don't sign the order!"*

But understanding the reader's emotional levers will allow you to manipulate them for your benefit. In Chapter 1, we discussed emotional response and intent response. This is where we actually get to generate them.

Which emotions can you target?

Salespeople will often talk about greed and fear. If you can target one of these in a client, it will help your sale. Clearly, if you are writing a sales document, this will still be true. Here's a list of common emotions you could look to tap into and the emotional/intent responses created:

- **Greed** – "I'll do it because I get something in return."
- **Envy** – "Everyone else is doing it, I must too."
- **Fear** – "If I don't do it, I'll suffer."
- **Pride** – "I'm the only one who can do it."
- **Pity** – "Those poor people, I must do something."

■ **Guilt** – "I'm the cause of all this, I should do something."

■ **Anger** – "How dare they! I'm going to do something about it."

■ **Happiness** – "I'm so happy, I'll do anything."

■ **Hope** – "If I do this, there's a chance of a positive result."

In this book, I've got a fairly dry subject to sell. I'm trying to keep you happy by writing in a chatty, light-hearted way, in the hopes that you'll keep reading and the information will sink in.[3] If I tried to play on your fears of catastrophe if you didn't read the book, I don't think you'd believe me. So picking the right emotions to target requires a good understanding of your reader.

Emotive words

You can manipulate your reader into an emotional state by using emotive words. For example, if I wanted to prey on your guilt about climate change to encourage you to buy products off my eco-website, I might use words like 'damage', 'harm', 'catastrophe', 'global', 'suffering' and 'responsibility'. I would then want to give you hope that your actions can change things. This would require words like 'action', 'help', 'difference', 'act now' and 'save'.

Once you know your reader and your intended result, use the emotions list above to work out the most appropriate emotional response. Then, write a list of emotive words that it may be useful to include. A word of caution: if your audience is very bright, you may need to be subtle in how you apply the words, otherwise you risk being seen as manipulative.

Rule 2: toy with people's emotions for your own ends

---

3 If you are still reading this, I guess that means it's working.

Loaded words

Loaded words are a specific type of emotive word. These are words with connotations beyond their meaning. If you describe a competitor's product as 'competent' or 'acceptable', readers will assume there is something wrong with it, despite there being no negative comments. Other examples include:

> *"The merger was* aborted.*"*
> *"His performance was* adequate.*"*
> *"She used* chemical assistance *to run that fast."*

 Loaded words are an extremely powerful way of subtly manipulating a reader. Again, don't over-use them for fear of your reader spotting their use.

Agitate, empathise and solve

This technique is a great example of exploiting emotive language. The first step is to describe the problem the reader has. Use emotive words to make the reader really 'feel' their problem. At this point the reader is at an emotional low. They will now be ready for two things: understanding and help. Empathise with the reader and show you understand their situation. This helps build your credibility and establishes common ground. Make sure you show you understand *their* particular problem, not the problem in general (see 'FABU' below). Finally, show you have a solution. By doing this, you put your reader in an emotionally vulnerable state and gain their trust, making it much more likely that they will accept your proposed solution. This approach is often used for healthcare products:

> *"Severe acne can be devastating for a teenager. The embarrassment, social rejection and resulting isolation can ruin young lives. We understand these problems and have dedicated our careers to solving them.*

The result of years of research, our groundbreaking new acne treatment will help you rebuild your life."

YOU, WE, I – GETTING PERSONAL

This is another sales mantra that is very useful in persuasive writing. Any persuasive conversation can be approached in this way, for example:

> *"Julie, **you** have been doing an excellent job on regional sales. **We** have been given a new target to increase them by 20% and **I** would like **you** to take charge of this."*

This order puts the subject first, then looks at a partnership and finally takes into account your opinions. This makes the reader's opinions/situation appear most important and puts your needs at the end of the text, making the reader more open to persuasion. Also, it reminds you as a writer to consider your audience from the start, which is never a bad thing.

In sales documentation, the order of word importance is the same. 'You' should be mentioned a lot, to focus the document on the needs of the client. 'We' should generally be used when speaking on behalf of your company and about your partnership with the client; and 'I' should be avoided, unless a personal opinion is required.

Let's look at a real example:

> *Helping **firms** to implement innovation as a robust and continuous business tool to develop ideas for new products and services.*

> *In partnership with regional, national and EC government agencies **we** provide access to over 10,000 scientists and engineers to develop*

the technology needed to realise these ideas and helping to share the costs of innovation through partnerships with other companies.

There is only one personalisation in this paragraph, and that is a 'we'. The only reference to any reader is the generic 'firms' on the first line. If you read this paragraph, it doesn't speak to you; it simply states things. A quick re-write gives us:

*AceCorp can help **you** innovate **your** products and services, and help **you** discover the power of innovation as a business strategy.*

*AceCorp provides innovative concept development across industry. **We** also provide access to over 10,000 scientists and engineers to develop the technology needed to realise these ideas. **We** can even help **you** share the costs of innovation through partnerships and government support.*

This is still dominated by 'we' (or the company name) but this is to be expected on a company website. However, it is much more personal, talking directly to you as the reader and discussing how 'we' can help 'you'.

Rule 3: talk directly to the reader using You, We and I

The only time you should ignore this rule is if you are required to write in the third person (e.g. academic papers, newspaper reports).

FABU

FABU is a useful acronym to show the difference between what something is and why anyone would care. FABU stands for:

- Features
- Advantages

- Benefits
- U-Appeal.

Features are the factual elements of a subject. Features give the subject *advantages* over other alternatives. These advantages then provide *benefits* to the users. The particular benefits that appeal to an individual are the *U-appeal*. Let's take this book as an example:

- **Feature**: Persuasive Writing Flowchart.
- **Advantage:** all the key points for basic persuasive writing on one page.
- **Benefit:** no need to hunt through the book looking for useful information.
- **U-Appeal:** I'm very busy and don't have time to look things up.

When trying to persuade, remember the reader has no real interest in features, advantages or benefits, only in the U-appeal. It doesn't matter if a TV has a 50-inch screen, which allows for bigger pictures, helping you become more immersed in your movies, if your reader is really looking for a TV for their kitchen. If you understand what the reader wants and present only the features, advantages and benefits that apply to them, you will have a much greater chance of persuading them.

Putting this together into a business context, you may write something like this:

> "*Acecorp is the oldest widget manufacturer in Europe* (Feature), *meaning we have an unparalleled knowledge of our customers' needs* (Advantage). *Whatever the situation, Acecorp has a widget to match* (Benefit), *saving you time and money searching for a solution* (U-Appeal)."

For a different customer, the U-appeal may be slightly different:

> "*Acecorp is the oldest widget manufacturer in Europe* (Feature),

meaning we have an unparalleled knowledge of our customers' needs (Advantage). *Whatever the situation, Acecorp has a widget to match* (Benefit), *meaning you get the perfect, no-compromise solution and total peace of mind* (U-Appeal)."

Rule 4: tell your readers about the benefits to them, not just the features

STORYTELLING

Fiction writers don't have a monopoly on telling stories; all writers can do it. In a non-fiction story, we use the constructs of fiction writing to make text more engaging, exciting and better-paced.

Rule 5: tell stories to your readers

Reams have been written about this subject but we'll focus on two concepts here:

1 the seven basic story plots;

2 the seven basic story elements.

The seven basic story plots

A story plot is simply an overall theme that defines where the story is going. This ties in closely with our reader response – the plot should help us get the response we want.

Various people have made all sorts of claims for the number of plots that exist but I like this list by Christopher Booker the best:

1 **Overcoming the monster** – defeating some force which threatens (e.g. *Star Wars*).

2 **The Quest** – typically a group set off in search of something and (usually) find it (e.g. *King Solomon's Mines*).

3 **Journey and Return** – the hero journeys away from home to somewhere different and finally comes back having experienced something and maybe changed for the better (e.g. *Gulliver's Travels*).

4 **Comedy** – not necessarily a funny plot. Some kind of misunderstanding or ignorance is created that keeps parties apart, which is resolved towards the end, bringing them back together (e.g. *A Midsummer Night's Dream*).

5 **Tragedy** – someone is tempted in some way (vanity, greed, etc.) and becomes increasingly desperate or trapped by their actions until at a climax they usually die (e.g. *Hamlet*).

6 **Rebirth** – hero is captured or oppressed and seems to be in a state of living death until it seems all is lost. Then, miraculously, they are freed (e.g. *Sleeping Beauty*).

7 **Rags to Riches** – self-explanatory really (e.g. *Cinderella*).

So how does this relate to persuasive writing? Consider writing an article for the popular press about a project you are working on. You could just relay the facts but people expect more in such articles, so why not tell them a story? Maybe your project has overcome great adversity to get where it is; maybe it is like a quest for knowledge; perhaps some misunderstanding meant it started badly before it was all sorted out. All of these could make interesting constructs for your facts, giving the reader much more than just information.

The seven basic story elements

As well as a plot, your story needs certain features which the audience can relate to. The following list is based on one by the screenwriter Robert Tobin. Not all these elements will be appropriate in all writing, but some will:

1 **A hero** – the main character, through whose eyes we see the story unfold.

2 **The hero's character flaw** – a limitation that hinders the hero, rendering them imperfect.

3 **Enabling circumstances** – the situation the hero is in at the start of the story, which maintains the hero's character flaw.

4 **The hero's ally** – a companion to the hero who will help them overcome their character flaw.

5 **An opponent** – a character who prevents the hero getting what they want. This opposition might be conscious (the 'bad guy') but can be unavoidable.

6 **The life-changing event** – A situation, usually created by the opponent, which causes the hero to react and try to force a change. This reaction usually involves the hero's flaw.

7 **Jeopardy** – something the hero must risk when responding to the life-changing event and overcoming their flaw. If there is no risk, there is no excitement to the story.

Again, what's this got to do with persuasive writing? Consider our business article example under the seven basic story plots. If we want to tell a Quest story (plot 2 in the previous list), the story elements may be:

1 Hero – the company or research team.

2 Character flaw – perhaps a lack of knowledge or expertise.

3 Enabling circumstances – low budget or other restriction.

4 Opponent – government.

5 Ally – another research team from another company.

6 Life-changing event – a withdrawal of funding by government.

7 Jeopardy – the decision to team up with rivals to share the development costs.

The end result may look something like this:

> It is Acecorp's (Hero) mission to develop treatments for the less publicised diseases and provide them to those least able to pay for their healthcare. To do this, we rely on government (Opponent) grants (Enabling circumstances) to bring in key expertise missing (Character flaw) from our core team. Suddenly, in early 2010, this government funding was cut (Life-changing event), putting our entire research effort in jeopardy. To continue our good work, we needed a radical solution and found it in the most unlikely of places. Greedcorp (Ally) have unparalleled expertise in tropical diseases but have previously only worked in niche, commercial medicines. We realised we could both benefit from collaboration (Jeopardy) and this most unlikely of marriages will guarantee we can continue to help the world's most vulnerable people.

Remember, you don't have to include every story element; pick the ones that best suit the situation.

There's a lot to remember in these first two sections, so, to help out, there's a checklist in Appendix 5 that can be used as a pre-writing tool to make sure you've covered all the bases.

PERSUASIVE WRITING EXAMPLE

The following is a real example and hence requires the back story. This abstract was written for a research proposal applying for grant funding. It was the day of the deadline and I had about half an hour to squeeze the proposal into a persuasive abstract (getting my excuses in early!). As a result, this is a 'warts and all', single-pass document produced under pressure. However, it still demonstrates how persuasive techniques can be used, even when the clock is against you.

The proposal was to develop a portable asbestos detector, so there was a clear health angle that could be used to create an emotive response. The abstract follows a problem-solution structure, in keeping with the proposal itself.

Asbestos-related diseases are the leading cause of occupational death in Europe. 500,000 European workers, mostly within the construction, demolition and remediation industries, are expected to die by 2030. Despite a ban on asbestos use, our members' workers are continually exposed to this potent, invisible carcinogen from legacy products such as insulation, water tanks, ceiling panels, floor tiles and textured wall coverings. We feel that this level of risk is completely unacceptable for our members and must be addressed.

Currently, asbestos is detected by a slow process of air sampling, with samples sent off to a lab and results being returned days later. Not only is this too late to take action, but tests are only performed if asbestos is suspected to be present. There is currently no way to detect asbestos in real-time. The ALERT project will change this.

A decade ago, researchers discovered a way to detect asbestos fibres through a light-scattering technique. This work stalled due to technical and cost barriers; barriers we now believe we can overcome. We have assembled a world-leading consortium to extend this early research and develop a low-cost portable detector that can be worn by the worker to continuously monitor their work environment.

By developing the ALERT system, we will provide 30 million European workers with a means of detecting asbestos the moment it is disturbed, allowing them to protect themselves and avoid becoming one of the 100,000 people worldwide killed each year by exposure to asbestos.

OK, so why is this persuasive? Let's break out some of the key elements:

Asbestos-related diseases are the leading cause of occupational death in Europe.

This is a fairly short sentence (12 words) containing a high-impact problem. By keeping it short, the reader is given time to digest the true seriousness of the problem before reading on. The next sentence in the abstract puts some meaningful scale to the problem. The primacy effect (see Chapter 3) should ensure these points stick with the reader.

potent, invisible carcinogen ... We feel that this level of risk is completely unacceptable

Here we see emotive language used to increase the impact. Carcinogen is a heavily loaded word and the use of the phrase "completely unacceptable" in an otherwise calm and measured paragraph suggests a genuine anger at the situation and passion for its resolution.

There is currently no way to detect asbestos in real-time. The ALERT project will change this.

We are into the middle of the text now and, even in this short abstract, our readers' attention is dipping. By using short, direct sentences, it keeps the reader alert and makes these critical points stick. To further help the readers' attention, the paragraphs are kept short, giving more time to digest information and more start and end points, helping with recall.

A decade ago ...

This is the technical bit, which also justifies why we need the funding. I used a storytelling approach to this paragraph, giving the history to the proposal. Despite its importance, we want the decision to be an emotive one at this stage, meaning this information shouldn't be in one of the prime locations. Anything three-quarters of the way through the text is least likely to be recalled, so this information goes here.

avoid becoming one of the 100,000 people worldwide killed each year

Here we are showing the benefits of the project in relation to the problem posed. In particular, we are hinting at what will happen if the project isn't funded. The subtext is, if you don't fund this project, you've got to answer to those 100,000 people's families. We can't say this outright in this type of document so this is the closest we can get without losing credibility.

I'm delighted to say the proposal secured funding for the project, which is now developing this fantastic piece of technology.

SUMMARY

The most persuasive writing will manipulate the audience. Take advantage of the following techniques to create emotional and intent responses in your readers:

- Consider how you can use Ethos **(respect)**, Logos **(reason)** and Pathos **(emotion)** to persuade your audience.
- Using **emotive language** to create different feelings.
- **Talk directly to the reader** and try not to talk about your opinions. Persuade them by identifying the benefits that appeal to them in particular.

- **Tell stories** to your readers. Choose a plot and include story elements to give structure to your writing and make it more engaging.

Remember:

Reason, Respect and Emotion = Reader Response = Result

3

Persuasion – Beyond Logic

Sometimes, the conclusion we wish our reader to reach is not necessarily the most logical one. If people were as logical as machines, the only way to persuade someone would be through cold, hard facts. Humans are, however, emotional animals and this greatly affects our ability to make rational decisions. This section talks through some of the mental biases which cloud our logic and explains how the knowledge of their effects can be used to make your writing more persuasive.

A note on references

You will notice the following examples do not contain references. Nor have I included lengthy anecdotes or details. This is purely to maximise the value of this book. There are plenty of great popular science books that provide all the details on decision-making theory and I would recommend reading a few. However, this book is very much about the practical application of the theories, not their provenance. For all the evidence, I suggest:

Sutherland, S. (2007), *Irrationality* (Pinter & Martin)

Lehrer, J. (2010), *The Decisive Moment* (Canongate Books).

THE SCIENCE OF DECISION-MAKING

The human brain is a marvel of evolution. It contains 20 billion neurons capable of running at 2,000 Hz, and can complete 100 million instructions per second. It takes in and processes billions of pieces of information every day and uses them to make life-or-death decisions in the blink of an eye. However, the very features that enable the brain to do this make it susceptible to all sorts of persuasion. Understanding how to exploit these features is the key to effective persuasive writing.

The human brain is a neural network (NN) and a key feature of NNs is the way they learn. NNs are particularly good at comparison between two scenarios – one observed and one remembered. For example, artificial NNs are used in object recognition as they can recognise something even if it is at a different angle or partially hidden. Because of this, NNs must learn before they can function and, the more experience they have, the better they can make decisions. By using experience-based decision-making, humans can very quickly assess an entire scenario without having to analyse it piece-by-piece.

Take football. In order to score a goal, a robot working on computer logic would need at least a genuine football and a goal before it could recognise the situation and take action. A human can kick a can through two jumpers because their brain can approximate, even when the perfect situation isn't available. This sort of information processing is not only fast, it means a decision can still be made when some information is missing. Whilst a computer will always win in a pure number-crunching task, it is no match for the human brain out in the real world.

However, this stunning decision engine still has its flaws. First, it uses chemicals such as adrenaline, testosterone and oxytocin to bias or 'switch' decision-making modes. Sometimes, the mode chosen (e.g. 'fight or flight') is not the best one but it's very hard to consciously override it. Secondly, the brain has no way of assessing the quality of completely new information and, once filed away, it becomes the benchmark. Finally, to make quick, firm decisions, the brain has to bias the information it receives and the way it uses it. If the bias is wrong, it can reinforce a bad choice.

PRIMACY – WHY COMING FIRST MATTERS

What is it?

Who was the first US president? Who was the second? Being first matters when it comes to memory. Imagine being handed documents to file. You take the first document and file it in the right place. Meanwhile, the next has already been handed to you. By the time you get round to looking at this, the next is passed on, and so forth. Chances are, the first few documents will end up in the right place and, after that, a fair few will be lost or misfiled. This is a fair analogy to what happens in the human brain. In any sequence, information at the start is always more likely to be remembered than information in the middle. You can see this effect really clearly with song lyrics:

And the rockets' red glare, the bombs bursting in air,

Gave proof through the night that our flag was still there.

Which famous song are these lines from? If you can't get it, here's the first line:

O! say can you see by the dawn's early light

I'm guessing most of you will now have spotted it's 'The Star-Spangled Banner'. This is typical for almost any poem and the majority of songs. Of course, looking at song lyrics also gives us useful clues for coping with primacy. For example, the chorus uses repetition and catchphrases to make it more memorable. The easiest songs to learn have short verses with familiar patterns (look at most Beatles songs).

Sometimes, we don't want everything we're writing to be memorable. The parts of your document are just like real estate locations. There are prime locations (start and end, headings, impact boxes) and sink estates (about three-quarters of the way through, in the middle of body text). Make sure your best points are housed in the nicest places and the things you don't want the reader to remember are moved to the mid-document slums.

Not only does the brain remember early information better, it puts greater weight on it. In order to carry out comparative decision-making, it needs a starting point. Information presented early is thus more likely to be stored as the reference data and, as explained below, remembered as 'right'. If you can make a convincing argument early, contradictory evidence is less likely to be believed.

Using primacy

The executive summary is the most common example of primacy. By telling the reader all the important points early, they are more likely to be remembered and believed. The same principle applies to lists and sequences. The third quarter of a document or sequence is the dwelling place of the controversial, the boring and the embarrassing. Put the information you don't want to be remembered where it won't be remembered.

AVAILABILITY

What is it?

Imagine you are in a small aeroplane 10,000 feet above the ground. You are about to make your first tandem skydive. The door is open, your legs are dangling over the edge and the countdown has begun. You may be trying to calm your nerves by remembering how safe skydiving is and how the instructors jump ten times a day and wouldn't do it if it were dangerous. However, all your brain can do is think: falling is bad. Falling a long way is worse, which makes this fall very bad indeed. The sight of the ground is more **available** than the safety statistics, so will tend to dominate your thinking. This is called 'the availability error'.

Availability can come about in a number of ways. Primacy and recency are both examples of availability, i.e. the information is more likely to dominate your thoughts by coming first or being seen most recently. Shocking and unexpected information is also highly available. Take the example above. If the person jumping before you had a parachute failure, what are the chances you'd jump? Their accident is both recent and shocking, making it highly available, even though it has no real statistical relevance to your safety.

Our own experiences will always tend to be more available than statistics or other people's experiences, meaning we will often prioritise this information over more reliable evidence.

Using availability

The best way to exploit availability is to make your points as available as possible for the reader. This can be achieved through the following:

1 **Presentation**. Use bold, informative headings, impact boxes (boxes containing key points to help them stand out), repetition of information, summaries and concise writing to increase information availability.

2 **Shock tactics**. Use unexpected and hard-hitting information

to override rational decision-making. Health and safety films rely on shock tactics to carry their message, as the audience is unlikely to do something that inconveniences them unless the consequences are readily available.

3 **Reader experience**. Personal experiences are always readily available so, if you know your reader well, use their experiences to reinforce your point of view. If you don't know your reader, you can guess at common experiences. For example, almost everyone will have a fond memory of the seaside. If you want to build a leisure pool in Milton Keynes, you could strengthen your application by linking positive memories of the seaside to the positive aspects of the leisure pool. After all, who would want to deny the residents of Milton Keynes just a taste of those experiences?

4 **Anecdotes**. Even if you can't link to personal experience, your reader will find it easier to relate to someone else's experience than they will to statistics. A good story is remembered and recalled more easily than data, making it more available, even if the data contradicts it. Let's say you make burglar alarms. A new government report has shown that burglaries have fallen 20% this year. There's no point trying to contradict this evidence so you need to make the threat of burglary more available to your customers. You can do this by providing anecdotes about crimes committed locally, especially against people of a similar age or social class (so the reader can relate better). If the crimes are violent (and hence shocking), the anecdotes will become even more available.

CONSISTENCY AND WHY WE HATE CHANGING OUR MINDS

What is it?

There is a whole series of interconnected psychological factors that all boil down to one thing: we hate being wrong. First up is **cognitive dissonance**. Humans are very poor at holding two or more conflicting beliefs. Therefore, if something comes along that challenges a belief, they must either abandon their old beliefs or make the new evidence fit them. This latter process is called **rationalisation**. This is further hampered by the human desire for consistency, making it very hard to change long-held beliefs. To make sure we avoid challenging our beliefs, we tend to seek out evidence to support them (**confirmation bias**) and we will cling to a bad decision if we have invested time and money in it (**sunk-cost bias**). In short, it takes a lot to get us to change our minds.

These traits can be seen most prominently in conspiracy theorists. Any evidence that contradicts their beliefs is avoided, assumed to be wrong or manipulated to fit. The longer a person believes the conspiracy and the greater their investment, the less likely they are to change. There are many examples in business and everyday life as well. Consider the manager who backs a new product that has poor sales. The evidence of poor sales conflicts with his belief that it is a great product, creating cognitive dissonance. The thought process will look something like this:

- "I can't cancel it now, we've invested millions in it" (sunk-cost bias).
- "Cancelling it will make me look weak and indecisive" (consistency).

- "Sales were probably down due to the very wet weather in May" (rationalisation).

- "Sales are 20% higher than in January!" (confirmation bias).

You sometimes wonder why people cling to their beliefs even in the face of overwhelming evidence against. It turns out your brain actually rewards you for finding a way to stick with your convictions, even if that requires illogical twisting of the evidence. This is what makes persuading someone with strong opinions so difficult.

It is likely the brain developed to prevent cognitive dissonance simply as a way of getting things done. In early human development, decisiveness was vital (e.g. fight or flight) and constant analysis of the options could be fatal. Also, it could be assumed that too many bad choices would also be fatal. Therefore, once a belief was formed, it was probably a good idea to cling to it. Although our lifestyles have changed, our desire for consistency remains the same.

Using consistency

As a writer, you can create dissonance or assist with rationalisations. The former is generally much harder. Let's revisit the new product example above. You need to write a recommendation to the manager suggesting the product line is cancelled. By understanding the decision-making biases above, we know that the manager:

- won't want to be wrong;

- won't appreciate being told he's wrong;

- will remember selective statistics that support continuation;

- won't want to read the arguments against;

- won't want to feel he has wasted time and money.

You can counter these objections by writing your report to minimise dissonance and address these objections. Some options include:

- The manager wasn't wrong at the time, circumstances have changed.
- You are pointing out the circumstances, not the mistake.
- Predict the ways the statistics could be misinterpreted and present alternative views to counter this.
- Draw him into the document by presenting the optimistic past before showing how events have changed.
- Show the savings he will make by being decisive and cancelling now.

The most important point is to challenge the idea, not the person who holds it.

Another way you can help break consistency is by using an analogous situation. For example, describe a decision with the same key features but in a non-business domain (e.g. buying a new kitchen). Your reader is likely to come to the right decision in the analogy. If you can then show how clear the parallels are, they are more likely to change their minds on the main decision. This is because you are reducing the narrow focus on the current situation and opening up the decision to comparison with other experiences. This extra internal evidence is more likely to convince them to change their mind than simply repeating your arguments. Of course, they may eliminate any cognitive dissonance by making an illogical decision in the analogy, in which case I suggest you immediately try to sell them a kitchen ...

Of course, you may be in favour of continuing that product line, even though it is failing. In this case, you need to ensure the entire report can be interpreted as positive by the manager. Moving complex analyses to the appendix, showing money invested so far instead of future savings and providing ready-made rationalisations will all help achieve the desired effect.

By understanding the likely problems thrown up by cognitive dissonance, you can plan ahead and write your text accordingly. However, it is essential you understand your reader. For example, using an aggressive argument to someone with very strong views is more likely to reinforce those views than to change them.

JUSTIFICATION AND EVIDENCE

What is it?

In order to make rational decisions, we need evidence. You can present facts and leave the reader to make up their own mind. However, it is more common (and less risky) to suggest a course of action and then explain why it should be followed. We do not like to make irrational decisions as it causes problems with our immediate and future justification of them, so we will always look for reasons why we have made a choice. This can be referred to as the Power of 'Because'. In fact, the 'because' does not even have to be rational to be effective. An experiment by Ellen Langer looked at queue-jumping at a photocopier. It seems people are just as likely to let you get away with it if you have a logical reason ("because I'm in a rush") as if you have an inane reason ("because I have to make copies").

Humans like to make rational decisions (rational to them at least) and the brain is easily satisfied. If it has a justification and doesn't have time to dwell on its validity, it doesn't seek further evidence. In fact, it will then rationalise the decision itself and seek out supporting evidence (see Consistency above). Since most decisions we make turn out to be right, this technique speeds up everyday decision-making and allows us to get things done.

As explained in the introduction to this chapter, the human decision-making process relies on comparison. If we have no reference points, facts become unusable. For example, knowing the price of an object is £50 does not give us any evidence about its value; we need to compare it with other similar products or with the proposed benefit to use it as evidence in our decision. Interestingly, we compare choices on a proportional basis and will often make different choices in different scenarios even when the net benefit is the same. If offered a £5 discount on a £10 item for driving 10 miles, most people would accept. However, if they were offered a £5 discount on a £100 item for the same 10-mile drive, most would say no, despite the actual monetary reward (£5 for driving 10 miles) being the same. Even if there is no better offer available, the 10-mile drive is seen as too much effort for the percentage discount offered in the second example.

Using justification and evidence

Justifications can be used to 'bury' bad news, especially when combined with confirmation bias. For example, presenting sales figures, you could explain:

> *"division 1 was 20% ahead of target, division 2 was 20% behind target and division 3 was on target."*

However, this begs the question as to why division 2 was behind target. An alternative would be:

> *"division 1 was 20% ahead of target, division 2 was slightly behind target due to adverse trading conditions, and division 3 hit its targets."*

Here, not only have we provided a 'because', we have eliminated the percentage associated with the bad news and made achieving targets sound better. As most of this document's audience don't want to hear bad news, the justification is sufficient.

We can use the preference for proportional comparison to pick best how we present our argument compared with the alternatives. For example, if one division has increased turnover by £2 million and you have only achieved £1.5 million, you would still be seen to be more successful if your percentage performance is better.

SIMPLICITY

What is it?

Isn't it nice when life is simple? Like most animals, we are driven to seek the easy life. If you have a choice between a perfectly cooked venison steak and catching your own dinner, you're unlikely to set off into Richmond Park with a crossbow. When things get really complicated, we become desperate to find an easy answer. Lose weight by dieting and regular exercise? No thanks, I'd like to take a pill that does it all. This is why, despite all common sense, the Nigeria scam still works.[1]

Of course, the same is true in the world of business. Millions of books worth tens of millions of pounds are sold each year promising to tell you how to make money. Business books are a great example. Consider these bestsellers and their implicit messages:

■ *The 4-Hour Workweek* (Timothy Ferriss) – "you can live a dream life like me by following these rules".

---

1 If you've never heard of the Nigeria scam, contact me, as I've got £1 million to move out of the country and you can keep 10% if you help.

- *Good to Great* (Jim Collins) – "to have a great business, just follow these simple rules".
- *Blue Ocean Strategy* (W. Chan Kim and Renee Mauborgne) – "make the competition irrelevant with this simple process".
- *7 Habits of Highly Effective People* (Stephen R. Covey) – "develop these habits and you'll be highly effective".

Despite all their undoubted good advice, the world isn't awash with millionaires who applied the books' techniques. Because the books seem to suggest success is straightforward, we buy them, read them, and wait for the money to roll in. In reality, you need to combine the advice with hard work and more than a bit of luck. Our brains are so desperate to take the perceived short cut, however, we convince ourselves the latest business bestseller will hold the key to success, despite failing to become a millionaire after reading the last 30.

Of course, it is clear to see why we have evolved this way. There is no point in expending any more energy than is necessary in achieving a goal so we should try and take short cuts wherever possible. Where we tend to fall down is in putting too much faith in the likely success of a short cut. Our animal ancestors didn't need to deal with deception very often; if they saw a short cut it was probably worth taking. In the modern business world, deception is everywhere and, all too often, we want so much to believe that we end up wasting our time and money.

Using simplicity

Your reader will want to believe what you have to say if the reward comes at very little cost to them. This may be financial, time or effort cost. This effect is even more pronounced if it takes effort away from the reader or provides a personal rather than a business benefit.

One of the programmes I often work on pays for leading research companies to do work on behalf of small companies. This is a fantastic scheme and is hence very difficult to get into. However, companies will routinely over-estimate their chance of success and spend excessive amounts trying to obtain this 'short cut'. On some of the smaller schemes, I have seen companies spend more than the grant would be worth chasing this dream.[2]

Simplicity is best used for short-term relationships with long-term results. Examples include selling books, self-help seminars, business strategy advice and training. It also works when offering solutions to complex or tedious consumer problems such as financial management, domestic chores and anything involving long-term maintenance. Because of the long-term nature of the results, your reader has to trust the benefits will appear. If the benefits seem great enough, they will convince themselves you can deliver these results, even if the actual odds are still huge.

Remember, this is more than just U-appeal. You are offering the miracle cure that solves the problem.

LOSS AND REWARD — A BIRD IN THE HAND ...

What is it?

As a rule, humans prefer to have things than not to have them. This is why greed and envy are such powerful emotions. This leads to some seemingly irrational behaviour.

---

2   Sunk-cost bias is also a major factor.

First, we tend to over-value what we have, especially if we think other people might want it. This in turn makes us much more afraid of losing something than of missing an opportunity to gain. A case in point is gambling. Although 68 per cent of people in the UK gamble in some form each year (Gambling Commission, 2007), the proportion of moderate or high-risk gamblers, i.e. those who value the potential gains higher than the potential losses, is just 2 per cent. This makes sense from an evolutionary perspective, where taking unnecessary risks could harm your chance of survival.

A similar principle applies to rewards. People tend to choose a small reward now over a bigger reward in the future. This is why free gifts are so successful – you get a quick hit now, rather than waiting for the benefits of a better product to emerge over time. Research has shown that, if there is a significant perceived difference in time before a reward becomes available, a quicker, smaller reward is chosen over a slower, longer one. For example, people offered £10 today over £20 a week later tended to take the smaller amount. If the time proportional difference is less, the bigger reward gets chosen (£110 in seven months over £100 in six months). This latter effect shows the influence of the brain's preference for proportional decision-making. Brain scans have shown reward choice is due to conflict between the rational and emotional parts of the brain. If emotion wins, you get less sooner.

This mental process appears to be another survival instinct. If you have something to eat now, it is less risky than the promise of more to eat in the future, as you have no guarantee you will actually get the reward.

Of course, it's not just long-term rewards that are sacrificed for short-term gain. Credit cards exploit our desire for short-term rewards and our inability to weigh that against long-term cost.

A similar subconscious argument goes on when making buying decisions. If the brain sees something it wants, it stimulates the release of dopamine, a chemical strongly associated with reward. If it then sees an associated cost, the dopamine is suppressed, reducing the pleasure felt. Interestingly, this mental argument is entirely subconscious but strongly influences your seemingly rational conscious decisions. Because the brain loves to feel happy, it can sometimes make irrational decisions to get a dopamine 'hit'. For example, how many times have you gone shopping and bought something you didn't need because you 'had to buy *something*'? This is the brain becoming fed up with seeing lots of things it can't have so insisting you give it something to feel happy about.

Of course, with any purchase you have to cope with buyer's remorse. This is the comedown from the dopamine high where you question your decision. Don't panic though, you'll soon rationalise it and start feeling good again.

Using loss and reward

Humans are loss-averse, even when the rewards are potentially significant. Therefore, avoid asking your reader to gamble, as most won't. If you have to, try to play down the costs and promote the benefits. Conversely, you can prevent risk-taking by highlighting the potential losses. You can make suggestions, but let the reader work it out for themselves. People don't like to be told they should or shouldn't do something, especially if it involves risk.

If you need to persuade someone to commit to a long-term payback, consider if there are any shorter-term alternatives, as these are likely to have a natural advantage over your proposal. If you can offer a short-term incentive, you will increase your chances of success.

With buying decisions, you need to excite the 'benefits' (pleasure) part of the brain without over-exciting the 'costs' (pain) part. If something is seen as a bargain, the pain of making the buying decision is reduced and the decision becomes easier. Remember, this is a subconscious decision before any rational analysis is brought in. If you can make the cost seem low, even if it isn't, the subconscious brain will start jumping up and down like a spoiled child demanding the conscious brain buy them a present. If the conscious brain, like a harassed parent, doesn't have the time to think about the decision too much, the subconscious will get its way and you will have persuaded the buyer.

OUTSIDE INFLUENCES – FOLLOWING THE HERD

What is it?

How does the brain make a decision when it doesn't have first-hand experience? The answer is to rely on the experience of others. This comes in the form of **social proof**.

There is nothing more powerful than a recommendation from someone you trust. Testimonials and quotes can be extremely persuasive. For example, when deciding who should receive an award within your company, a glowing reference from a client is likely to carry much more weight than the candidate's own claims. It all comes back to ethos – use the reputations of people your reader trusts. Social proof is usually in the form of quotes, support and case studies.

A number of factors make social proof so powerful:

■ **Evidence** – if you haven't experienced something first-hand, you rely on others to experience it for you and feed back the results.

- **Experience** – you will place most trust in the opinions of people you believe can make the most informed assessment.

- **Conformity** – most people don't like to be different so will choose the most popular option.

- **Aspiration** – if someone you admire recommends something, you will trust that recommendation as you aspire to be like your idol. Celebrity endorsements continually exploit this.

Sometimes, social proof can be seriously abused. Theatres have occasionally quoted critics out of context to promote plays, leading to confusion and disappointment for those misled. A typical example comes from the Wyndham Theatre in 2009. For their production of *The Shawshank Redemption*, they posted a reviewer's quote calling it:

> *"A superbly gripping, genuinely uplifting drama."*

What the reviewer actually said was:

> *"The 1994 film ... is a superbly gripping, genuinely uplifting prison drama about friendship and the power of hope ... In almost every respect, the stage version is inferior to the movie."*
>
> Charles Spencer – *Daily Telegraph*

Without means to check, most people assumed it was genuine praise for the play from a respected critic. In many cases, this was sufficient social proof to convince them to buy.

Social proof doesn't have to rely on genuinely experienced third parties offering advice. If you can place the reader in someone else's shoes and see a situation from another point of view, they will begin to feel they understand the situation and will make decisions based on that understanding. This effect can be so great that people can sometimes become convinced they had the experience themselves.

Using outside influences

This book is a great example. I suspect there will be quotes on the back of the book praising its qualities. I also expect they will look something like this:

> *"An excellent summary of the key elements of persuasive business writing"*
>
> (Dr Alan McNamara, NHS Innovations)

> *"Accessible, readable and wonderfully useful. This book is a must-read for all our staff"*
>
> (James Hall, CEO, Pera International)

Glowing reviews, I'm sure you'll agree. The quotes are persuasive as they come from people who sound knowledgeable and credible as sources of opinion.

But what if you can't find the very highest calibre of social proof? Well, you can use the perception of experience to boost your document's credibility. In the examples above, the first person quoted is based on a personal friend and the second is based on the CEO of the company I work for. In the absence of any impartial reviews by knowledgeable well-known people, I have relied on creating the impression of credibility through the job titles. You end up seeing recommendations from a 'Dr' and a CEO of an international company and (I hope), are suitably impressed. Of course, the downside of showing you this is I now can't use these people on the back cover of this book ...

You can also use weight of numbers to spark a desire to conform. A typical example from advertising is:

"80% of people we surveyed said they would recommend Gleemex to a friend."

Social proof can even come about via association. Quoting people the reader admires talking generically about your subject matter is still persuasive, as the reader seeks to avoid a conflicting opinion with that held by the idol, even if they are not talking about your product/service in particular. For example, if I wanted investment in my company, I might use the following quote on the document:

"Today is absolutely the time to invest in our most promising technology companies"

(Lord Drayson, Science and Innovation minister)

Clearly Lord Drayson is not talking about my company, which may be a terrible investment. However, the famous name and relevant quote will add credibility to my request for funds.

REPETITION, REPETITION, REPETITION

"We shall fight on the beaches, we shall fight on the landing grounds, we shall fight in the fields and in the streets, we shall fight in the hills, we shall never surrender."

(Winston Churchill)

Good repetition is reiterating the main points of your argument more than once and, preferably, in multiple different ways. The more experience the brain has, the more chance there is it will recall it and assume it is correct. Most importantly, Winston Churchill used it so it must be good!

ANCHORING – DECISION-MAKING ALL AT SEA

What is it?

I have to confess I haven't tried this in a document but I was so fascinated by its potential I thought I'd include it here. The anchoring effect suggests the brain becomes obsessed with pieces of information when making a decision, whether that information is relevant or not. A range of experiments has shown we will over-value or under-value items depending on the size of other numbers present in the same discussion/document. An example looks something like this:

Hitachi 4 series TV. Standby power less than 1 watt. 2 × 8 W speakers, 7-day programme guide, just 18 kg. Save 33%, now only £399.99.

Hitachi 42-inch full 1080 p TV. 500 cd/m² brightness, 178-degree viewing angle, 1060 mm visible screen. Was £600.00, now only £399.99.

The anchoring effect suggests the lower ad would appear a better bargain, as the reader is confronted with a series of large numbers which contrast with the relatively modest size of the price. The top ad presents small numbers, making the price seem large by comparison.

Despite the complete irrelevance of the earlier numbers, they still have a subconscious effect on our decision-making. This is because the brain is constantly on the search for comparison data with which to make an informed decision. When genuinely useful data isn't available, the brain fixates on irrelevant but available information.

Using anchoring

The example above is a great place to start. If you know you have to present an unpalatable number such as a high price, make sure it is preceded by lots of other numbers significantly bigger, and vice versa. For example, if you need to present a disappointing survey response of say 50 per cent agreement, precede it with other, lower, results, even if they aren't relevant to any decision.

THE HALO EFFECT

What is it?

Humans like consistency and prefer the simple life. Simplifying complex things such as personality is achieved via 'the halo effect'. If a person or organisation has a strongly positive (or negative) trait, we will assume that is representative of their overall nature. Without wishing to name names, there are a number of prominent performers, adored by their fans, who also happen to be violent drunks, rapists, racists and drug addicts. In anyone else, these traits could not be ignored, and would most likely be the most memorable feature of that person. However, when someone has a very strong positive feature, such as musical talent or acting ability, this overrides almost any other consideration.

Celebrity is a particular example of the halo effect. Because someone is famous, it is assumed they are a 'good' person. This links back to social proof, where celebrity endorsement is so effective, despite the high likelihood that the celebrity's opinion is otherwise meaningless.

The same principles apply to businesses as well as people. In recent years a company, famous for its high end toasters, launched a new range of kettles into the UK market. Despite the fact it has no history of making kettles, you would assume its reputation for other products means its kettles would be equally good. According to extensive online reviews, however, this is really not the case.

The halo effect works in reverse as well (commonly called 'the horns effect'). If a person is ugly, they are assumed to be bad or stupid (try to spot the intelligent, attractive villains in children's stories). If a company's website and marketing material are poor, you assume the products are rubbish. Imagine if the company above had made kettles first and then launched its toaster range. Do you think anyone would buy them? We don't want the complication of something 'bad' having good aspects; it's easier just to label the whole lot together.

Using the halo effect

Clearly, you can exploit the halo effect directly – if you have good traits, make sure your reader is reminded of them, even if they aren't relevant to the current situation.

One of the easiest ways of exploiting this effect is in presentation. There is an assumption that if something looks good, it is good. Why do supermarkets try so hard to get perfectly red, round tomatoes? It's not to make their displays look pretty, it's because consumers assume these taste 'better' because they look 'better'. Chapter 9 gives some useful advice for improving the appearance of your documents.

In a competitive scenario, you need to remove your rivals' halos and get rid of your horns. In the case of your rivals, present their weaknesses anonymously before revealing who they belong to. Allow the reader to decide they don't want what's on offer from a company like that before they can be swayed by the halo effect and the host of other biases that come with it. You can even acknowledge your rival's reputation to heighten the disparity between the perception and reality (e.g. "amazingly, this comes from the supposed 'experts' in the field, Acecorp"). The same principle can be applied to get rid of your horns. Get the reader to want your offering before they know it's yours. After that, the biases will start to work in your favour.

Shell used this approach in a series of TV adverts. The majority of the ad showed a committed environmentalist doing his thing, before revealing he worked for Shell. Before Shell's name is mentioned, few would condemn the character shown. Once his virtue is established, it acts to remove the oil company's horns.

RECENCY – THE HERE AND NOW

What is it?

We started this chapter with primacy. Unsurprisingly, recency is the opposite. The recency effect says you are most likely to remember the last thing you heard. This is perfectly logical, as it is fresh in your mind. However, recency will bias experiences. We tend to assume that the last option is the best option. We can call this 'the crescendo effect'.[3] It may be a chicken and egg

---

3   My invention, but it sounds about right.

situation – are choices presented this way because of the effect, or was the effect created by the way people present information? No matter. The fact is the option people are most likely to choose is the last one presented. This seems to work best with a list of three choices, as three is not too many to make a snap decision. Four or more choices normally prompt the reader to think about their options a bit more.

Going off topic a bit, lists of three options have some other interesting effects. Imagine you have three choices. The first two are equally appealing. The third is similar to the first but worse. People will most often choose the first option rather than the second. This is the same no matter the order in which they are presented.

Let's say you have two choices of supplier to present to your boss, Acecorp and Zulu. You want Zulu but the bids are pretty much equal. If you list two deals from Zulu, where one of them is noticeably worse value, it is more likely your boss will pick the good deal from Zulu rather than the deal from Acecorp. For example:

- Zulu 1: £1,000 per 2.0 tonnes
- Acecorp: £1,100 per 2.2 tonnes
- Zulu 2: £1,400 per 2.4 tonnes.

The other strange thing about a list of three is that people are more likely to believe two things they've never heard before if they are bundled up with something they know to be true. It's truth by association. For example, if a customer knew you were the largest supplier in the UK, you could use this in a list with two other facts they may find more difficult to believe to increase their credibility.

Using recency

This is fairly straightforward. If you want someone to remember something, make sure it is the last thing they hear. If you don't want them to remember it, don't put it at the end (or the beginning for that matter).

THE READER IS ALWAYS RIGHT

There's a harsh reality to writing: the reader is always right. Even if the decision they make is not the one you wanted them to make, that's your fault, not theirs.

I've found this very hard to deal with in the past. When you are applying for a €1 million grant on behalf of a group of small companies, it is agonising to miss out. You rant and rave at the reviewers, blaming their ignorance, their inability to read and their wanton bias against you. While doing this, you completely miss the point: they based their decision on what you wrote.

You can think of the act of persuasive writing as a game. Sometimes you win, sometimes you lose. In any game, you don't blame the opposition for beating you ("how dare they be better than me, that's unfair"). Exactly the same thing applies with persuasive writing. The reader can only work on the information you present. Even if they hold very strong opposite views, you still have an opportunity to persuade them. If you fail, you can hardly blame them.

By arming yourself with knowledge of the reader's decision-making processes, you have a better chance of persuading them to make the decision you want and winning the game.

Rule 6: the reader is always right

SUMMARY

Primacy – people form opinions on first impressions and remember early information better.

Availability – information more easily recalled has more influence in decision-making.

Consistency – once people have made up their mind, it is very difficult to change it. This is due to:

- *Sunk-cost bias* – actual loss is more painful than potential loss.
- *Rationalisation* – your brain rewards you for twisting evidence to suit your existing views.
- *Confirmation bias* – you only seek out evidence that agrees with your beliefs.
- *Social pressure* – consistency is seen as strong.

Justification and evidence – people like to know why, even when the 'because' isn't particularly convincing; when deciding, it is easier to compare proportionately than exactly.

Simplicity – people constantly seek the easy life and will convince themselves of a potential short cut's likely success.

Loss and reward – we over-value what we have; if we make a quick decision we'll take the smaller, quicker reward; we aren't good at linking short-term gains with long-term cost; our brains do a crude subconscious cost/benefit analysis.

Outside influences – people will look to others to help with the decision; people are most influenced by experience, conformity and aspiration.

Repetition – find different ways to make the same point.

Anchoring – the brain will use nearby data for comparison if it doesn't have anything better.

Halo/horns effect – if you are well-known for one good trait, you are assumed to be good in other traits and vice versa.

Recency – the last thing read sticks in the mind; people are most likely to choose the last of three choices.

4

Commercial Break: Advertisement Slogans

Advertisements are a great place to find examples of persuasive techniques. In particular, advertising slogans are the distilled elixir of persuasion. Consider the following:

"Probably the best lager in the world" – Carlsberg

"Because you're worth it" – L'Oréal

"Does exactly what it says on the tin" – Ronseal

"Guinness is good for you" – Guinness

"The Independent. It is. Are you?" – The Independent.

These are all hugely effective slogans but use different techniques to get their message across. In the case of Carlsberg, it's the best. Ronseal works. *The Independent* makes the reader feel intelligent and part of an exclusive group. In fact, most advertising slogans fit into one of seven different categories:

▓ **Superlatives** – this is the best product

▓ **Does what it says on the tin** – this product works

▓ **Lifestyle** – this product is good for your health and/or happiness

▓ **Clever** – this product is for clever people like you

▓ **Challenging** – this product challenges all your preconceptions

▓ **Exclusivity** – you belong to an elite club if you have this product

▓ **Memorable** – you know the product, we're just reminding you.

Beyond slogans, advertisements in general are a goldmine of persuasive techniques. If you work in advertising, you will almost certainly analyse adverts from rival agencies and much of this will be familiar to you. If you don't, I would thoroughly recommend watching TV ad breaks to identify the strategies used. Then see if you can adapt the technique for the documents you write. Let's look at some examples from a recent TV ad break:

More Than car insurance – This ad is all about what you get free when you buy car insurance. This is exploiting our desire for instant reward – the whole package value may be worse than others but the up-front cost is made to seem much less. Whenever I buy car insurance, I love to see how much I've saved against my renewal quote and this ad taps straight into that desire. In the same break, a DFS sofa advert uses exactly the same technique, offering huge discounts and interest-free credit. This is a favoured technique for advertisers in highly competitive markets with expensive, low differentiation products.

Volkswagen Polo – Volkswagen know they are seen as an expensive brand so acknowledge and challenge that view in their ad. The ad is all about how you won't believe the Polo is such good value. This is a great example of challenging reader consistency by accepting their view and then showing things have changed.

Waitrose – Waitrose have gone down the social proof route and employed the chef Heston Blumenthal to front their ads. As one of the most famous chefs in the country, his view is respected and his association with the Waitrose brand will lend credibility to the brand within their target audience.

You can also do this exercise with sales letters, charity requests and printed ads.

Finally, further analysis of ads and their effectiveness reveals persuasive words, which can persuade by creating positive or negative emotions. The table opposite lists some words you could consider using in your text to trigger the appropriate positive or negative feelings in the reader:

Positive – words to inspire a reader to action	Negative – words to scare a reader to action
Novelty (newer is generally seen as better) – *new, discover, breakthrough*	Result – *catastrophe, disaster*
Reliability – *proven, guaranteed, safe*	Impact – *loss, suffer, pain, struggle*
Lifestyle – positive effects on: *health, freedom, easy*	Lifestyle – negative effects on: *health, freedom, business*
Greed – *best, free, results, save, offer*	Personal (talking directly to the reader) – *you, your, responsible*
Personal (talking directly to the reader) – *you, your*	Timeliness (when to act) – *now, soon, action, change*
Exclusivity – *limited, exclusive*	
Timeliness (when to act/expect) – *now, soon*	

Clearly, over-use of these words can make your document look more like a script for a shopping channel than a sales proposal. Don't be tempted to apply everything and say:

> *"Don't risk suffering the pain of catastrophic performance. Our break-through service is guaranteed to give you the freedom you crave. Get results now with our exclusive, limited time offer."*

Unless you do actually work on a shopping channel, of course.

5

Conciseness Equals Clarity

This section of the book focuses on making your message come through as clearly as possible. In most cases, this can be achieved by being concise.

The average introduction[1] for a practical business book is six pages. In this book, it's two pages. Why? My belief is that the majority of people want a short introduction to get a feel for the book's style before buying or reading on. I don't believe anyone will say of this book: *"the content was great but it really needed a longer introduction"*.

A definition of concise writing

Concise writing achieves the correct reader response in the most efficient manner.

Note: this does not mean that you remove every non-critical word; you are unlikely to persuade a vendor to lower their price by simply writing "give me a 10% discount".

Having said this, there are many cases where brevity is better. This chapter will look at:

- Eliminating jargon
- Cutting down on long words
- Reducing sentence length
- Cutting padding
- Culling lazy words
- Examples, similes and analogies.

Remember – if following a rule makes your writing less persuasive, break it.

---

1   All the body text up to the first chapter.

ASON AND THE JARGONAUTS

If you work in business, you will use jargon. Jargon is another way of saying 'business-specific language'. This doesn't make it bad; in fact, without it, it would be almost impossible to describe some of the things we do. Where jargon becomes a problem is when it starts to obscure the real meaning.

The consulting industry has gained a reputation as the worst abusers of jargon. Consider the following:

> *In an increasingly global economy where competing on price alone is no longer a sustainable business strategy, companies need to add value through innovation, differentiating their offering through new product features and process functionality.*

This company's clients are small businesses which have probably never had a sustainable business strategy, let alone thought about differentiating their offering. What they probably meant to say was:

> *In an increasingly global economy, competing on price alone is no longer an option. Companies can add value to their products and services through innovation, beating the competition through new features and functionality.*

Not a big difference, but an important one. The language is much more conversational and hence more accessible to those outside the industry.

Rule 7: cut out jargon your reader will not be familiar with

Writing how we talk is a great way to cut down on inappropriate jargon. If you can't imagine saying it to your audience, why would you write it to them?

> **Rule 8:** write how you would talk unless you have to be formal

Supersized words

Alongside jargon is the supersized word. Just as Morgan Spurlock suffered serious health problems from being fed a diet of supersized burgers,[2] so your reader will become sick if fed on a diet of overly long words.

I struggle with this. I'm proud of my vocabulary and want to show it off whenever possible. However, not everyone shares my passion for words. If I say 'belligerent' instead of 'aggressive', I've got to know my reader will understand. If they don't, they will probably think I am being pretentious or just not get my meaning at all. If your audience does not understand you, you can't persuade them. Appendix 2 contains a list of commonly used supersized words and some alternatives.

> **Rule 9:** only use words of three syllables or more if you cannot use a shorter alternative

As mentioned earlier, break the rules when you need to. Some long words impart a very specific meaning. 'Curmudgeonly' and 'cantankerous' mean bad-tempered, but tend to be used to describe old people, especially men. As such, they paint a very specific image in the reader's mind and could not be replaced without losing meaning.

Don't just think it is long words that confuse. Words like 'concur', 'viable' and 'deem' are all great words but may not

---

2 If you haven't seen the film 'Super-size Me', I would thoroughly recommend it. Don't watch it with a burger in your hand, though.

be suitable for your audience. Say 'agree', 'possible' or 'think' instead.

Words are like weapons. If you use a shotgun to kill a fly, you'll end up with an almighty mess on your hands.[3]

SENTENCES THAT ARE TOO LONG WITH LITTLE PUNCTUATION CAN CAUSE THE READER TO LOSE INTEREST IN YOUR WORK OR STRUGGLE TO EXTRACT THE MEANING RESULTING IN YOUR WORK BEING LESS PERSUASIVE

If the heading weren't example enough, consider the following:

An estimated 12 million man-days are lost annually to stomach bugs caused by bacteria growing in poorly stored product, difficult to clean portions of over & under counter dispensing systems used in food halls, restaurants, canteens & even in dispensing equipment in food processing plants throughout Europe. The main approach at present to minimise microbial growth is to use chill/freeze distribution & storage, but this method is costly, inconvenient, & potentially hazardous, with thaw/re-freeze risks all along the supply chain & risk at the 'point of delivery' through inadequate thawing & storage procedures & the practice of re-freezing unused product.

---

3   See 'Examples, similes and analogies' for more on analogies.

These two sentences clock up a staggering 100 words. By the time you've finished each of them, you've forgotten how they started. Bad punctuation doesn't help the flow either.

Rule 10: don't write sentences that require you to take a breath in the middle

As with all the rules, there are caveats. Punctuation can be used to allow for breath pauses; if the sentence has a high pace, you can cram a lot of words in. As a rule of thumb, however, you should average around 15–20 words per sentence.

Rule 11: vary sentence length

Note the word 'average' in the text above. If all your sentences are the same length, the effect can be very hypnotic. That may be your desired effect but, in most cases, sending the reader to sleep is a bad thing. Due to its style (short, punchy, concise), this guide is currently running at an average of 10 words per sentence. However, this paragraph's sentences are 8, 14, 19, 20, 14 and 10 words respectively. This makes the paragraph rise and fall, changing its pace.

Another rule for sentences is to keep them to one main point. Your reader is unlikely to remember more than that, even in a short document. You'll find this naturally keeps your sentence length down as well. If you find you have a long sentence with multiple points, see if you can split them up.

Rule 12: include one main point per sentence

So, now we know this, let's revisit the paragraph about stomach bugs:

In Europe, an estimated 12 million man-days p.a. are lost to stomach bugs. These are caused by bacteria growing in poorly stored product and dirty dispensing systems in food halls and restaurants, and even in dispensing equipment in food processing plants. Currently, microbial growth is minimized through chill/freeze distribution & storage. However, this method is costly, inconvenient and potentially hazardous, with thaw/re-freeze risks all along the supply chain. Inadequate thawing & storage procedures at the point of delivery make matters even worse.

This paragraph now averages 16.4 words per sentence, with sentences ranging from 11 to 28 words. This, along with a few other tweaks, makes for a much more readable paragraph, subject matter excepted of course.

Sentences can be even shorter than 11 words. In fact, they can be as short as one word. See? Punctuation gives the reader a chance to breathe, pause and reflect. Very short sentences can be used to create high impact by forcing the reader to stop and absorb the meaning of those few words. Remember: conciseness brings clarity.

THE WRITER'S DIET – CUTTING PADDING

When writing as you talk, a lot of text will end up being redundant. This is fine in speech but can become tedious on paper. The same problem occurs if you try to sound too official – the meaning can get lost in a blubbery mass of padding. Consider the following text:

The committee for future funding carefully and deliberately assessed the latest new information that was sent by head office. The committee felt that the suggestion for the team to revert back to the original set of guidelines on funding did not represent forward progress as the key recommendations by the board were no longer fully covered.

Not very elegant I'm sure you will agree. So how do you spot padding? Use these tips to apply the axe accurately.

Adjectives and adverbs

Rule 13: cut down on your adjectives and adverbs

Adjectives and adverbs describe nouns and verbs respectively.[4] Both are vital parts of language but over-use can make your writing stodgy. For example:

"I slowly, painfully analysed the long, thick, heavy document sent by the young, keen writer in the marketing department."

Tedious, isn't it? By selecting better verbs and nouns, you can get across the same meaning but in a more engaging way.

"I trudged through the tome sent by the bright young thing in marketing."

If 'tome' is too exotic, try a single adjective such as 'huge' in front of 'document'.

'The' and 'that'

Rule 14: keep 'the' and 'that' to a minimum

---

4   See 'Grammar refresher' in Chapter 6.

Often these words are redundant in a sentence. For example:

"The director of AceCorp said that the new accounting system would eliminate the errors and the delays that have occurred recently."

Eliminate a few excess words, a swift bit of re-jigging and you end up with:

"Acecorp's director said the new accounting system would eliminate the recent delays and errors."

Adjective before noun

Rule 15: adjective before noun

No one talks about the 'machine for milling' if they can say the 'milling machine'. By placing the adjective in front of the noun, you cut your word count and increase clarity. So remember, don't use the rules for concise writing, use the concise writing rules.

CULLING LAZY WORDS

This may seem a little harsh, but your paragraph is not a charity. Only the fittest, strongest and best words should survive your editing process. Anything else should be ruthlessly dispatched.

Unfortunately, there are no hard and fast rules for this one. However, here's an example to help you spot that layabout language:

I would like to point out that the received document was only received on the 24th October. Can I draw your attention to the terms of the contract, which clearly state that the document transmission should be completed by the 20th October at the latest. I sincerely hope that this contractual issue will not occur in the future.

OK, what can we change? Having said there were no rules, there are some guidelines. Look out for:

- repetition or redundant phrases;
- making something simple sound impressive;
- flowery niceties.

Note: repeating key points throughout a document is good practice. Just make sure the repetition is well spaced.

In this example, *'received'* is repeated so we should be able to remove one of them. Also, the contract comes up twice so we should look at that. *'Document transmission should be completed'.* That sounds to me like someone trying too hard. Out it goes. *'I would like to point out'* and *'can I draw your attention to'* are definitely in the flowery niceties category.

Remember: Reader Response equals Result. The aim of this text is to tell the reader off and make sure the problem does not occur again. However, there are no consequences if it does, so maybe we need to add that. If we really want to achieve our objectives, we could write something like:

The document arrived on the 24th October. The contract clearly states it should have arrived by the 20th October. If any further documents are delayed, we will take our business elsewhere.

Although it has a direct tone, this is appropriate for a letter of complaint. With all those lazy words gone, you end up with a paragraph that really means business.

As always, break the rule to be more persuasive. Words that seem redundant can in fact be vital to creating a persuasive atmosphere. If this were not the case, adverts would say "Buy Brand X soap, it's cheap and gets you clean". Since they don't, we can assume there is some value in some redundant words. All you need to do is question each phrase carefully to see if you really need it.

Rule 16: cull any words that don't help persuade your reader

EXAMPLES, SIMILES AND ANALOGIES

It may seem strange to talk about analogies and examples in a section on conciseness. However, remember our definition of concise writing:

Concise writing achieves the correct reader response in the most efficient manner.

This book is littered with examples because it is much easier to show redundant words than to describe them. As discussed in Chapter 3, the brain is a neural network. Neural networks learn through relating events to existing experience patterns. If you can compare a new piece of information with an existing pattern, the brain is more likely to understand it.

Rule 17: use examples and analogies to improve your readers' understanding

For business writing, the most useful forms of comparison are:

Examples: surely I don't have to give an example of an example? To be honest I'm not even sure how ...

Similes: these describe one thing being *like* another. For example, *"he walked off like John Wayne"*. This is much faster and more evocative than describing exactly how he walked.

Metaphors: these state that one thing *is* another. These tend to be used more in literature than formal reports but still have their place. For example, in Chapter 6, the verb is described as *"the workhorse of any sentence"*. Clearly it isn't actually a horse, but the phrase is more punchy than saying *"the verb in a sentence is the word that produces the action and so can be said to 'do the work' in a sentence"*.

Analogies: like similes, these are used to show similarities between two things. Generally, an analogy will provide more detail on the similarities than a simile, allowing you to make more obtuse comparisons. For example, *"he wrote like a bad knife-thrower – if the punctuation did hit the page, it usually stuck in the wrong place, with predictably painful results"*.

A SEVEN-STEP CONCISE WRITING PROCESS

This is a process you can follow to draft and edit documents when you have strict page or word limits. You may also find this works well for you in general writing. It was developed for writing bids for a UK government programme. Each section was strictly limited in length, meaning conciseness was king. However, the document still had to be persuasive; this was a funding competition after all. Although it doesn't include all the techniques discussed so far, it covers enough for everyday use.

Step 1 – Bullets

Plan your document using your favoured technique (see Chapter 8). Get to the point where you have a list of section headings. Complete each section in bullet-point form, with each bullet expressing only the most important points.

Step 2 – Story

Check your bullet points to make sure they tell an effective story. Is there a better order to make the points in? Have you missed a logical step?

Step 3 – Expand

Draft out the document, adding as few words as possible to the bullet points to make complete sentences. The vast majority of added text should be supporting facts, not new parts to the story.

Step 4 – Read each sentence in isolation

- What does it actually say? Could this be misinterpreted?
- Do I need to say this? Does it add value?
- Are there other points made in the sentence that are not the main point? If so, can I remove them or move them into a separate sentence?

Step 5 – Read the section as a whole

Do the sentences flow together? Has adding words modified the story?

Step 6 – Close edit

Use some or all of the following techniques:

- Summarise – can one word or phrase replace a list of similar items? Look out for the word 'and', as this is sometimes an indication of unnecessary additions.
- Eliminate unnecessary jargon – would an **ignorant genius** understand it?
- Edit for sentence length – try to keep the average sentence length under 20 words and provide lots of variation.

If you have time:

- eliminate unnecessary adjectives/adverbs;
- remove 'the' and 'that' where possible;
- remove repetition – especially in multiple uses of the same description.

Step 7 – Re-read and proofread

Go away for a bit, come back and read straight through, out loud. Read in reverse and look for spelling/grammar errors.

A worked example of the writing process can be found in Appendix 7.

SUMMARY

Concise writing means being persuasive in the most efficient way possible:

- Take out unnecessary **jargon** and overly complex words.
- Keep your **sentences** to one main point, keep the average length down and vary their length.
- **Cull** any words that don't help you be persuasive.
- Use **analogies and examples** to explain yourself more accurately and concisely.

This chapter has mainly covered editing techniques. Beyond learning the skills, the next most important is to **know when to stop editing**. A business document is a tool. If you need to drive in a nail, you need a hammer. You don't need a top-of-the-range, perfectly balanced, laser engraved hammer. Stop editing when the document is good enough to do the job. After that, you're just engraving your hammer.

6

Verbs Equal Vigour

The verb is the workhorse of any sentence. Without a verb, nouns would just sit around doing nothing. Adjectives may be able to tell you how wonderful the noun is, but it's still sitting on its backside (actually, it's not even doing that, as 'to sit' is a verb). Chuck in a verb, however, and your sentence is jumping, skipping, singing, dancing and even racing across the page (or just sitting on its backside …).

This section will look at:

■ names of words – a grammar refresher;

■ activating passive verbs;

■ freeing nominalised nouns.

Remember – if following a rule makes your writing less persuasive, break it.

GRAMMAR REFRESHER

If your only contact with grammar is when you visit her in the care home, this is the section for you.

When I started looking into this, I found there was a lot of grammar. Books full of it. Too much of it, in fact. I've broken most of it in the last few sentences as well. Which goes to show, to write persuasively, you don't need lots of rules. In order to explain the text below, however, we need to review some basic word types:

Noun – names a person, object, place or idea/feeling.

Examples: Professor Plum, candlestick, billiard room, murder.[1]

---

1   Murder is both a noun and a verb: "He committed murder" (noun) or "He murdered her" (verb).

Pronoun – word that replaces a noun or partners a noun to show possession.

Examples: it, them, they, mine, theirs, ours.

Adjective – adds information on the features of a noun or pronoun – answers the questions "what kind?", "which one?", "how many?", or "how much?".

Examples: <u>studious</u> Professor Plum, <u>heavy</u> candlestick, <u>dark</u> billiard room, <u>brutal</u> murder.

Verb – describes an action or state of being. Note: the verb 'to be' is not descriptive and so requires adverbs to create action.

Examples: run, skip, play, follow, chase, shoot, bore, annoy.

Adverb – adds information on how, when, where, or to what extent the verb performs.

Examples: run <u>quickly</u>, skip <u>nearby</u>, play <u>tomorrow</u>, follow <u>closely</u>.

VERBS JUST WANNA HAVE FUN

Verbs are all about action and energy. By choosing the right sentence structure, you give more energy to your verbs and they in turn will give more energy to your writing. Before we get on to the advice, however, we need just a bit more background grammar.

Sentences are made up of a **subject**, a **verb** and, usually, an **object**. The subject of a sentence is the 'who' or 'what' the verb relates to. For example:

Subject Verb   Object
<u>Jenny</u> <u>tripped</u> over the <u>table</u>.

The person or 'thing' that performs the action described by the verb is called the *agent*. In the example above, Jenny is both the subject and the agent in the sentence, i.e. she is the one who tripped and the one who performed the action of tripping. Where a sentence is arranged agent – verb – object (as above), it is said to use the *active voice*. Generally, sentences read better if they are in this order. This is because the reader likes to find out:

Who did what to whom ("the salmon leapt into the air")

rather than:

What had something done to it by whom ("the air was leapt into by the salmon").

You can hear how clumsy that sounds if you read it out loud.

In the second example above, the subject of the sentence (the air) is not the agent (which is the salmon). Where a sentence is arranged subject – verb – agent, it is said to use the *passive voice*.

Although this sounds a bit complex, there are some easy ways to spot the use of the passive and active voices. Passive sentences use variants of the verb 'to be' (is being, was, will be, etc.) and also tend to have the word 'by'.

Rule 18: favour the active voice wherever possible

Example:

Subject   Verb   Agent
"The <u>house</u> was <u>painted</u> by the <u>decorator</u>" becomes:

"The decorator painted the house".

If the agent is not present, you may need to add it:

Subject   Verb
"The <u>report</u> was <u>submitted</u> on time" becomes:

"We submitted the report on time".

It may be harder to spot passive verbs in longer phrases:

Subject   Verb   Agent

"Little <u>attention</u> <u>is paid</u> to drug addiction in prisons by the <u>authorities</u>" becomes:

"The authorities pay little attention to drug addiction in prisons".

Sometimes, the passive voice is useful and so there are exceptions to this rule. Use the passive voice when:

- the emphasis needs to be on the object (*"A fire was started by a gang of youths"*);
- you don't know who the subject is (*"A man was murdered yesterday"*);
- you don't want your subject to take responsibility (*"All staff are expected to work overtime"*);
- the writing style dictates it (e.g. academic papers).

However, if your text doesn't require one of the exemptions, activate your verbs and let them have fun.

VERBS IN DISGUISE – NOUN SUFFIXES

There's nothing crueller than to suppress a verb. A nominalised noun is a verb that has been imprisoned within a noun. They can usually be spotted by the addition of the following endings:

-ion   Participate – Participation

-ment   Entertain – Entertainment

-ance   Perform – Performance

-ence   Obedient – Obedience

-ure   Sign – Signature

Examples:

"We would appreciate your <u>signature</u> on the contract" becomes:

"Please <u>sign</u> the contract".

"Jane's <u>performance</u> was poor" becomes: "Jane <u>performed</u> poorly".

"The <u>implementation</u> of changes is the divisional manager's responsibility" becomes:

"<u>Implementing</u> the changes is the divisional manager's responsibility"

Or, even better:

"The divisional manager is responsible for making changes".

In some cases, verbs can sound harsh and nominalised nouns can help soften the impact (e.g. "we would appreciate your assistance" is much gentler than "please help"). However, in doing this, they suck energy from the sentence. Which statement would a charity use in an advert, for example? Set your verbs free and your reader will thank you.

SUMMARY

- Verbs give life to your writing and should be used wherever possible.
- Arrange sentences Agent – Verb – Object to use the **active voice**.
- Arrange sentences Subject – Verb – Agent to use the **passive voice**.
- **Favour the active voice** unless you are sure it's not appropriate.

- Try to **convert nominalised nouns** back to their original verbs.

- Remember – a piece of writing is there to do a job: In most cases correct grammar improves clarity and keeps the reader happy but **don't be afraid to bend the rules** if it makes your writing more persuasive.

7

Mistakes

The worst way to get things wrong is to make a stupid mistake. Demonstrating this perfectly, a recent CV arrived with a section entitled EDUCTAION.[1] Another candidate listed 'attention to detail' and 'excellent English' as key attributes, despite their CV being littered with mistakes. Still, if you are going to fail at getting a job, you might as well get it over with before the interview. Of course, I bet there'll be a mistake in this chapter now …

Mistakes to look out for:

- Commonly confused words
- Using the wrong word
- Scattershot punctuation and no punctuation
- Poor spelling
- 'Mistakes' that aren't mistakes.

COMMONLY CONFUSED WORDS

Next to misuse of the apostrophe (which we'll come to), word confusion is right at the top of most readers' list of pet hates. Here are the most common examples and how to get them right:

Its/It's: with this pair, the apostrophe does not indicate possession, it indicates that there is a letter missing (the 'I' in 'it is').

> *"It's warm today."* **NOT** *"Its warm today."*

> *"I bought a new car and broke its wiper."* **NOT** *"I bought a new car and broke it's wiper."*

DO NOT rely on grammar checkers in word processors – mine got the example above wrong! We should really make that a rule:

---

1 Spell checkers normally ignore words in block capitals, so be careful.

Rule 20: DO NOT rely on grammar checkers in word processors

There/Their: another common one, 'there' indicates a location, 'their' indicates possession. So:

> *"Their house is over there." NOT "There house is over their."*

Practice/Practise: The verb has an 'S' and the noun has a 'C',[2] so:

> *"I will practi<u>s</u>e to be able to run a dental practi<u>c</u>e."*

Principle/Principal: a principle is a moral or belief. Principal means first or major. It is also a name for some leaders (e.g. in colleges), so:

> *"My princip<u>les</u> are the princip<u>al</u> reason for not becoming a Princip<u>al</u>."*

Affect/Effect: affect is a verb and only ever a verb.[3] It means 'to change or alter' something. Effect can be a verb or a noun. If a verb, it means 'to bring about'. If a noun, it is a result. So:

> *"I tried to <u>effect</u> a change in my job, but the <u>effect</u> of this has been to severely <u>affect</u> my performance."*

Course/Coarse: coarse is rough, crude or as in coarse fishing. Course is something you go on (assault course, teaching course). So:

> *"I went on a <u>course</u> about <u>coarse</u> fishing but the instructor was very <u>coarse</u>."*

i.e./e.g.: i.e. means 'id est' and is used to provide an explanation; e.g. means 'exempli gratia' and is used to introduce one or more examples. So:

---

2 In US English, you can also use practice for both the verb and noun.
3 Except in psychology, where affect refers to experiencing a feeling or emotion.

"The car had many good features, e.g. legroom, acceleration and han-dling. Its boot was adequate, i.e. it could fit my golf clubs in."

Both e.g. and i.e. are preceded by punctuation (usually a comma) but are not usually followed by punctuation in UK English.

Just a note on the use of 'e.g.' and 'etc.': 'etc.' is used to end a truncated list, rather than completing it; 'e.g.' introduces one or more examples. As a result, it is not appropriate to use etc. at the end of a list of examples started with 'e.g'.

There are many more commonly confused pairs of words so, if in doubt, check in a dictionary.

At this point, it is worth mentioning UK vs US spelling. Despite sharing the same origins, they are different. For example:

- -ise (UK) vs -ize (US), as in analyze (US), or criticise (UK), although both are fine in UK English;
- -ou (UK) vs -o (US), as in color (US), favorite (US) or armour (UK);
- -re (UK) vs -er (US), as in centre (UK) or theater (US);
- -ogue (UK) vs -og (US), as in analogue (UK) or catalog (US).

Generally, unless you are American, stick to UK English. If you are writing in English but outside the UK, use whichever version you are most familiar with but stick with one version – although the reader will understand, it is still bad form to mix versions.

USING THE WRONG WORD

Take a look at the clipping below:

Dive in!

Egypt is your gateway to the Red
Sea's underwater paradise. See
hammerhead and whale sharks,
including many indigenous species.

At first glance, there's nothing wrong with it. However, they've used the word 'indigenous', which means native. When you know this, the joy of finding species native to the Red Sea, in the Red Sea, is somewhat diminished.

Or take this example:

> With a relatively flat hierarchy, it ensures that irrespective of the authoritative status of the source – the issues can be escalated to the appropriate authority and eventually discussed amongst the project board. At this stage, the relevant partner representative on the board can give sound input to any decisions that might be made, however the project board as a whole shall have the penultimate decision.

This reads like a desperate attempt to make a very simple

paragraph sound important, and it has tripped up the writer. It is clear that the board should have the ultimate decision, not the penultimate one. Use of the word 'final' would have avoided this error. Sometimes, trying to use big words just means you use the wrong one, through accident or ignorance.

Beyond failed attempts at sounding impressive, the biggest source of incorrect words is typographical errors (a slipped finger typing the wrong letter but forming a recognised word). This leads us to another rule:

Rule 21: don't rely on word processor spell checkers

Why? Because incorrect words are not spelling mistakes and so won't be picked up. As another CV explained:

"Work Experience: Dealing with customers' conflicts that arouse."

Nice work if you can get it.

SCATTERSHOT PUNCTUATION AND NO PUNCTUATION

Lets' start this section with an example! If you use: too much punctuation, in the wrong place; you will find that your document is: hard to read!!?. On the other hand if you use no punctuation you will also find that your reader will struggle to follow your thought processes especially if as is often the case you include asides or other additional information.

Although the paragraph above is still readable, it is difficult to follow, so correct use of punctuation can really help a reader.

Rule 22: use punctuation sparingly and accurately

This calls for another grammar refresher. The main punctuation marks prone to misuse are commas, full stops, semicolons, colons and apostrophes.

The comma: the comma acts as a pause in a sentence. Examples include:

- separating items in a list (*"The colours were red, green, black and blue"*);

- cordoning off an aside (*"Sometimes, despite the temperature, I like to go skiing"*);

- placing supporting information before or after a statement (*"Although raining, the fete went ahead"* or *"The fete would go ahead, weather permitting"*);

- indicating to a reader where a pause for breath or dramatic pause may be (*"He opened the door, and then saw the body"*).

You'll notice from the examples above that the words on one side of the comma form a complete sentence, whilst on the other they don't. This is a good rule to help you decide when to use a comma and when to use a semicolon. With a semicolon, the words either side form two complete sentences, as you'll see below.

Note there is nothing wrong with a comma before 'and', except at the end of a list. An exception to this is if the last list item contains an 'and' as part of it: e.g. "personnel, engineering, and health and safety".

The semicolon: this mark looks like a combination of a full stop and a comma; and handily it is used where a full stop would be too abrupt but a comma would be too weak. The two parts of a sentence separated by a semicolon should be linked in some way. For example:

"Thank you for your recent letter; we apologise for the delay in replying."

Semicolons can also be used to separate lists. They are good at the end of bullet points or can be used in a continual list that contains commas:

"Our catalogue covers: ancient history, archaeology and myths; military history; royalty and the nobility; and modern history."

The full stop: a pretty easy one, it marks the end of a sentence and puts an end to a particular thought. Just. Don't. Over-use. Them.

The colon: this is mostly used to introduce lists or separate out headings on the same line (as here). However, colons are also used in two other circumstances:

1 to act as a 'drum roll' for a key statement in a sentence ("There's only one problem with importing it: it's illegal");

2 to separate two sharply contrasting items without the finality of a full stop or smoothness of the word 'but' ("Dave was able to complete his assignment on time: Warren wasn't").

The apostrophe: This is the leading cause of ulcers among English teachers. I've seen steam come out of their ears after seeing a shop advertising Bag's and Shoe's. So, to calm the nerves of English teachers everywhere, here are the basic rules:

The apostrophe is used to show two things: possession and contraction. Possession means that the word in question belongs to someone or something. Contraction means that a letter or multiple letters have been missed out.

"Dave's suitcase went missing. 'That's odd', said Dave."

In the above sentence, the first apostrophe shows that the suitcase belongs to Dave; the second replaces the 'i' in 'that is'. All very simple so far.

If the possessor of the word ends in an 's' (usually a plural such as 'boys' or 'trousers'), put the apostrophe after the 's' but do not add another. For example:

> *"The boys' trousers were broken. All the trousers' zips were missing."*

If just one boy had broken his trousers, it would be:

> *"The boy's trousers were broken. The trousers' zip was missing."*

If a word ends in 'ss', like 'boss', it would take 's to become boss's.

Last one for now. If you have a plural abbreviation or date (e.g. '1990s', 'SMEs'), don't use an apostrophe unless there is possession (e.g. "The SMEs' balance sheets were missing").

There are lots of other punctuation marks with their own rules but it would take many pages to cover them all. I'll leave you with the most important rule of all, though:

It is never right to use more than one exclamation mark!!!!!

POOR SPELLING

Unfortunately, no one can remember how to spell every single word in their vocabulary. Add to that typing errors and you will almost always get spelling mistakes in your work. At the start of this chapter we saw a couple of CV mistakes that almost certainly lost those candidates the chance of interviews. Good spelling is never an optional extra.

A word processor with a spell checker is extremely valuable but don't rely on it. Mine often changes languages without warning, flashing up correct words as mistakes. Also, their dictionaries are not perfect and they will only warn you about nonsense words, not correctly spelt words used in the wrong place.

The answer here is proofreading. You will never be able to spot all the mistakes in your own work, as you will skim read.

Rule 23: get someone else to proofread your work

In particular, look out for incorrect word use caused by the close proximity of keyboard keys. If you are writing about banking, there is little danger of saying something obscene, as all the keys around the 'B' produce nonsense words. If you are writing about a cricketer out for a duck, however, be careful of the letters either side of the 'D'.

A top tip is to read each paragraph in reverse. This takes the words out of context and stops you skim-reading them.

It is also vital you get an audience representative to read your work. This is someone with a personality as close as possible to your intended audience. They will help you spot situations where you've written for an audience of one (see Chapter 1). For example, in the first draft of this book, I referred to Machiavelli.[4] One of my proofreaders said, "Who's Machiavelli?" At that point I realised I had to take the reference out – I wasn't writing for my audience but for myself.

---

4 An Italian philosopher and writer who wrote *The Prince*, a political treatise advocating cunning, deceit and blunt realism in politics.

'MISTAKES' THAT AREN'T MISTAKES

The following are all perfectly allowable in English writing. If you don't believe me, look at any book on plain English or grammar:

1 Starting a sentence with 'But' or 'And'.

2 Ending a sentence in a preposition (for, to, in, about, etc.). There's no such rule in modern English grammar.

3 Splitting infinitives (putting a word between 'to' and the verb, for example: "to boldly go where no man has gone before"). The *Oxford Guide to English Usage* recommends you avoid splitting your infinitives but says it's perfectly fine if it improves the flow or meaning of the sentence.

4 Writing paragraphs of only one sentence.

And remember – if following a rule makes your writing less persuasive, break it.

SUMMARY

Embarrassing mistakes can completely prevent your message getting across.

▪ Make use of **spelling and grammar checkers** but don't rely on them.

▪ Watch out for **incorrect word use**.

▪ Understand how to **punctuate**.

▪ Get someone else to **proofread** your work.

8

Planning and Structuring

One of the hardest aspects of writing is getting started. Equally difficult is knowing when to stop. I'm aiming to keep this book brief, so if it goes much over 40,000 words you'll know that I can't teach you anything on this second point.

This chapter will introduce simple techniques to use when planning your writing; structures to help you present information; and the phases to go through to ensure a timely final draft. It will consider:

- Planning, drafting and editing
- Readability statistics
- Document structures.

PLAN, DRAFT, EDIT

Actually putting pen to paper (or fingers to keys) is only one part of the writing process. First of all, you have to know what to write. Unless you are a writing prodigy, chances are your first draft will need some serious editing. Remember these aspects in your time planning and it will help a lot.

Planning your writing

There is a huge number of ways to start writing. However, most of the successful ones will use some form of structured planning process. These can be broadly divided into visual and analytical planning, which will probably suit right- and left-brained people accordingly.

Visual Planning

This category includes clustering, mind-mapping and other shape- and pattern-based techniques. Essentially, they all use the same principle: draw circles and/or lines to connect thoughts and keywords.

Start in the middle of a page with the core topic of your document. Surround that with all the thoughts you have on that topic. Next, use lines and shapes to link the topics and group them. Re-draft regularly to gradually shape your concepts into a formal structure.

An example of a visual plan can be seen below:

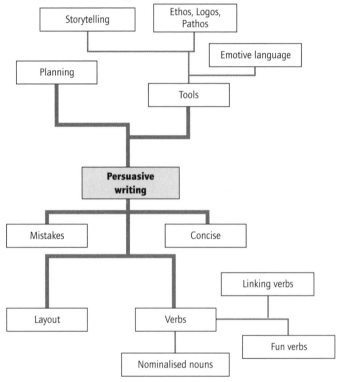

Any visual plan will eventually have to be turned into a list, which will form the structure of the document you are writing.

Analytical planning

This is just a fancy way of saying 'making a list'. I'm a big fan of paper lists but electronic lists are easier to play around with. Not much more to say on this, really.

With both these techniques, you will need some sort of structure to put your thoughts into. We'll cover this in a bit.

Drafting

Very simply, this is emptying your thoughts on to paper.

Top tips with drafting:

- Write 'Draft' at the top of your page. This reminds you that you don't have to be too careful.

- Once you start, don't stop. It takes more energy to get started again than to keep going.

- If you do have to stop, leave some prompts on the page so you know what to start writing when you come back.

- If you do not know what to put, leave a place holder. A place holder should have a distinguishing feature, a hint on what to put, and be highlighted, eg: >>>The thing about place holders<<<. Just make sure your place holders are visible: it is highly embarrassing to find place holders in text once you have sent it off, especially if they are rude about your audience.

- Consider setting a time limit on a drafting session to really focus your mind.

The drawback of pure drafting is that it increases your edit time, especially if you have word limits to adhere to. In these cases, consider bullet-point drafting as shown in the seven-step Concise Writing Process in Chapter 5.

Editing

This is all the stuff in Chapters 5, 6 and 7 of this book. Go through the whole document page by page, using your editing techniques to correct mistakes, tighten language and tidy up the structure.

Wherever possible, get someone else to at least read your work before it goes out. I do not know a single writer who is capable of spotting all of their own mistakes.

It is usually easiest to edit in stages, rather than trying to do the whole lot at once. A typical sequence is:

1 sentence and word length;

2 verbs;

3 spelling;

4 layout;

5 edit by another person.

Editing must be thorough – you can't skim-edit. Don't edit when you are in a hurry or distracted. Find a quiet room somewhere and set aside plenty of time.

Readability statistics

You may want to use readability statistics to help guide your editing. These are a feature of most modern word processors, giving you information on the 'readability' of your text. For example, Microsoft Word uses the Flesch Reading Ease and the Flesch-Kincade Grade Level. The first of these is a percentage score indicating how easy the text is to read. The second converts these scores into a US school grade. Effectively, this indicates how old a person must be to easily understand your text on the first read.

In order to convert to a simpler metric, add five to the grade level to get an age in years. Examples are shown below:

We are fundamentally opposed to the undiminished attempts by the dominant organisations to steamroller their unreasonable and anti-competitive offerings into the existing marketplace without appropriate consideration of the societal impacts. We will multi-laterally oppose any bullying of small to medium enterprises by larger organisations, especially when societal and environmental impacts may be detrimental to the national interest.

Readability: 0%
Grade level: 23.6 (age of 28.6)

The cat is red. I like cats. I want to stroke the cat. Do you like cats?

Readability: 100%
Grade level: 0 (age of 5)

WARNING! Readability statistics are only an indicator and must be used with your audience in mind. Bear in mind the following:

- **Match readability to the reading age of your audience:** The language in the second example above would be fine for a three-year-old but might be considered extremely patronising by an Oxbridge graduate. Likewise, more complex text may be beyond the abilities of a younger audience.

- **Assume all adults have a reading age of 18 unless you know for sure they don't:** If you know all members of your audience have a high reading age **and** will appreciate more complex text, feel free to write in a suitable style. If you can't be sure on both these points, assume they have the minimum 'adult' reading age, i.e. 18 (grade level 13).

- **Required jargon:** Statistics do not take into account required jargon. A medical report will always be called less 'readable' than a staff email, even if most of the supporting language is the same.

- **Bad grammar:** Statistics take no account of bad grammar. For example, a poorly punctuated sentence may be considered more 'readable' than a good one.

So, readability statistics are a useful guide but not a rule. If your text has a grade level between 10 and 13, you are probably fine for most business writing, assuming the grammar is reasonable.

DOCUMENT STRUCTURES

You may find that your planning phase reveals a natural document structure. Alternatively, storytelling may force you to order your sections in a certain way to get the effect you want. If not, the following may be relevant.

First, a general rule:

Rule 24: make your main point accessible

This doesn't mean always putting it first – just use headings, layout and structure to lead your reader to it quickly. Even with this, you may need to use one of the following structures:

- **Chronological:** ordered by time, most recent first for instant impact, old – new to tell a story.
- **Geographical:** by location, e.g. a review of global activities.
- **Problem – Cause – Solution:** fairly self-explanatory. Another good storytelling structure, drawing the reader in.
- **Question and Answer:** think of the six questions (who, how, why, when, where, what), pose them as headings and then answer them. Most commonly seen in Frequently Asked Questions (FAQ) on a website.
- **Simple to Complex:** start with knowledge the reader has, then gradually introduce new knowledge.

- **General to Specific**: present the big picture before providing the details on the specific elements of that picture.
- **Order of Reader Importance**: set the scene, drop the big news on them, then less important, then minor news. Most often used by, you've guessed it, the news.
- **SCRAP:**
  - **S**ituation: what is this referring to?
  - **C**omplication: what has gone wrong?
  - **R**esolution: how can it be fixed?
  - **A**ction: who needs to do what?
  - **P**oliteness: sign off in a friendly fashion.
- **SOAP:**
  - **S**ituation: what is this referring to?
  - **O**bjective: what is our aim?
  - **A**ppraisal: show the research/analysis done.
  - **P**roposal: what should be done in light of this?
- **The 5 Ps:**
  - **P**osition: where are we?
  - **P**roblem: what needs changing?
  - **P**ossibilities: what are the options?
  - **P**roposal: here is a suggested option.
  - **P**ackaging: here is how we go about implementing it.
- **Formal Report:**
  - Title
  - Contents
  - Summary/abstract
  - Introduction
  - Discussion

– Conclusions

– Recommendations.

If you are still stuck, go and have a cup of tea and come back to it later – something will come to you eventually.

SUMMARY

It is almost impossible to write without some combination of planning, drafting and editing.

- Find a **set-up that suits you** – one process does not fit all.
- **Readability statistics** are a useful guide but are only a guide. Remember your target audience when using them.
- When planning, the most important aspect is **structure**.
- If a natural structure doesn't emerge, use a **template**.

9

Layout, Fonts and Formatting

In some roles and professions, writing is simply about producing text. However, if you have complete control over the final document, you will need to consider formatting. This comes back to the whole 'Reader Response equals Result' thing. If you make it easy for your reader to find the information they need, they are more likely to respond in the way you want.

This chapter will consider:

- Font choice
- Layout
- Headings
- Bullets
- Tables and diagrams.

FONT CHOICE

Apparently, some fonts are easier to read than others. If you pick a font that is too decorative or too dense, your reader may struggle to extract your meaning and will lose interest.

A debate rages on the readability of different fonts, with various camps claiming benefits for serif and sans serif fonts. The difference is that serif fonts have little curly bits at the tips of the letters (serifs), whereas sans serif fonts are plainer. This can be seen clearly on the letter 'T' in the following examples:

The cat sat on the mat. *(Serif)*

The cat sat on the mat. *(Sans serif)*

In truth, there seems to be no difference in readability so it's your choice. Some research has shown that, for dense, printed body text, serif fonts are slightly more readable but this also depends on the audience.

As a general rule, most people are familiar with reading sans serif fonts from the screen and serif fonts in print. For younger people (and certain professions such as engineers), sans serif fonts are more familiar so it's very much a case of tailoring your font choice to your audience.

An area where sans serif fonts do have the edge is with impact. By dispensing with the twiddly bits, they are more striking and so are excellent for headings (as shown in this book) and emphasised text.

Example serif fonts (all 10 point[1])

Times New Roman – the most widely used of all serif fonts

Palatino Linotype – less dense than Times New Roman

Bookman Old Style – even wider than Palatino

Example sans serif fonts (all 10 point)

Arial – the most famous of the sans serif fonts

Verdana – commonly used on the internet, a very wide font

Microsoft Sans Serif - another popular font, although quite dense

---

1 The point size refers to the height of the letters only, not the width.

Which font should I choose?

The short answer is, it's entirely up to you. However, consider the document and its audience. Fonts that are too big will make it look as if you are writing for children. Fonts that are too small will be hard to read. Also, decorative fonts are fine for fête signs but not formal reports.

For A4 documents, 12 point Times New Roman is a fairly safe choice. Because of its size, this book uses a 10 point font, but one slightly wider than Times New Roman to make sure the page doesn't appear cluttered.

Don't be tempted to pick a small font if you have a word or page limit. Yes, Arial Narrow will get you far more words to the line than Palatino but it will be much harder to read. Instead, use concise writing to minimise your need for words.

In summary, font choice is very personal and there are plenty to choose from. Just make sure your audience can read it.

LAYOUT

There is one very simple rule with layout:

Rule 25: white space is your friend

This may sound strange but bear with me. White space helps to emphasise the text that is there. If you write reams of text with narrow margins, no line spacings, no headings and full justification, it will be very difficult to read. Consider the following:

Project No: 516319 PROJECT

demand for the product. We aim to demonstrate in this proposal that we have the critical mass of resources, expertise and market knowledge to be able to develop and exploit a novel, high performance monolithic chemical vapour deposition (CVD) diamond dosimeter array. Being able to offer such an exclusive, protectable product, will significantly improve the competitiveness of the SME consortium and ultimately a large number of wider SME supply chain and end users.

All of the SMEs in our partnership (electronics, semiconductors and dosimetry) have experienced growing pressure from globalisation and increased competition from low labour rate countries, especially from India and the Far East. It has also been increasingly difficult for us to win new business and retain existing customers as our customer base is increasingly seeking suppliers on a global basis. Pricing pressures are prevalent with a continuous demand to reduce prices, especially in the semi-conductor market. The Internet has allowed companies to source products and procure them world-wide as easily as sourcing locally. Major companies have worldwide agreements and dictate the price adder they will pay to local distribution/stockists. As noted by the European observatory for SMEs, [1] SMEs are more labour intensive than large enterprises; in order to produce the value of output, SMEs use more labour as input. SMEs are therefore more likely to be affected by competition in labour rates and the treat from this Globalisation. It is no longer sufficient for us to rely on QCD, (quality, cost and delivery) as our global competitors have demonstrated a near equal ability to compete on quality and delivery and a far greater scope to reduce cost through low labour rates. This is particularly true of dosimetry where the leading technologies, (ionisation chamber, silicon diode, photographic film) are relatively mature. The ionisation chamber for example, a mainstay of absolute reference dosimetry has its roots in 80 years of history. Like any mature technology, intense pressure from around the world, (particularly those regions with low labour rates) is affecting revenue and driving down prices.

We believe that we can only fight this globalisation in the supply chain by innovation in our products and services. We need to develop products that provide us with a clear differentiator in terms of performance, features and functionality. We need to move away from our dependence on shrinking domestic markets and further 'internationalise' our business. We see this project as being the perfect mechanism to achieve this goal by innovating our products beyond the reach of our non-European competitors. If approved, it will allow us to offer a more cost effective, faster, higher performance radiation dosimeter perfectly matched to the most recent demands of radiotherapy and that cannot be matched by our competition. We know the demand for the technology is extremely strong and growing rapidly, fuelled by the demand for conformal radiotherapy techniques such as IMRT. As IMRT starts to dominate radiotherapy, so will the demand for IMRT dosimetry. In section 2 we will demonstrate why there is no current solution available world-wide and how we will successfully achieve this. This also opens up the opportunity for us to move up the value chain, providing integration of systems rather than continue purely as a low value component supplier. If we are successful, we all intend (excluding of course the RTD performers and non dominant Large Enterprise - LE) to utilise the IPR developed to allow us to exploit the knowledge based economy as international licensors and penetrate other markets potentially on a global scale, through the sale of licenses. This will improve our competitiveness even further. We have a desire and ability to absorb the technology developed by the RTD performers into our own products, and use this to form a robust and effective supply chain. In short, not only will we be developing a dosimetry technology that is a world first and which the radiotherapy industry is demanding but we will be securing and protecting our future business.

1.2   Facilitation of Transnational Cooperation

Traditionally, SMEs rarely work with each other across National boundaries, as their markets, within supply chains have been traditionally domestic. The radiotherapy dosimetry market does typically involve more transnational cooperation than other sectors. However, the need for Trans-National Co-operation is further increasing due to the demand, by end-users for a regional supply capability into sites all over the Union and globally. We as SMEs also recognise the importance of transnational co-operation throughout Europe. With growing pressure on the dosimetry market from large enterprises in the USA it is the only way we can innovate our products to maintain our position as market leaders in our sector. Without transnational co-operation we are fragmented, with it we can establish the critical mass of scientific, technological and commercial resource required to stay competitive. For example, all the companies represented in this proposal have demonstrated the capability to innovate, however no single company has the pre-requisite scientific knowledge and expertise in CVD diamond production, neutron irradiation, sensor

Project No: 516319 PROJECT

1   Relevance to the Objectives of Cooperative Research

1.1   Improving SME Competitiveness

Cancer is the second leading cause of death in the world today. Throughout Europe, nearly 1 million people die each year from cancer and one in three European citizens can expect to contract the condition during their lifetime. The cost of cancer treatment in Europe alone is estimated to be in excess of €50 billion p.a., [ref 2-Medline]. By 2020 it is predicted that there will be 20 million new cancer patients each year. Radiotherapy is typically used to treat cancer in 1 of every 2 cases, with a success rate of approximately 50%, [2]. Indeed, recent advances in conformal Radiotherapy technology, such as intensity modulated radiotherapy (IMRT), have made significant improvements to the success rate in the treatment of cancer. These systems allow the radiotherapy beams to be temporally and geometrically shaped to match the tumour, maximising dose to the diseased tissue and minimising damage to surrounding healthy tissue. Ironically, these tremendous advancements in highly variable spatial and temporal resolution radiotherapy treatments have exposed significant weaknesses in conventional dosimetry. Conventional dosimetry techniques are not able to provide the resolution and speed of measurement required by IMRT, thereby dramatically limiting the number of people that can be treated. As will be described in detail later, this proposal aims to develop an innovative, radiotherapy dosimetry technology to improve the speed and effectiveness with which IMRT fields can be measured and then implemented. This will open up IMRT treatment for a far greater number of people.

So how will this proposal improve SME competitiveness? Small and Medium-sized Enterprises are recognized as playing a crucial role in European competitiveness and job creation. We represent the overwhelming majority of enterprises in Europe (99.8%) and create two thirds of all employment. As confirmed by the European Observatory for SMEs, 2000, [ref 3] the Medical Equipment sector is a sector dominated by SMEs, with 85000 enterprises engaged in the manufacture of medical, precision and optical instruments. With respect to major items of radiotherapy equipment such as linear accelerators, the market is dominated by large enterprises. This is of course to be expected with full IMRT system installation costing up to €1.2million. The clear market leader is the US company Varian, with a 56% of the total global radiotherapy market share, [ref 4: UBS Warburg LLC]. Other major players include Siemens (with a 23% market share) and the Swedish company Elekta (15% share). With the world market for radiotherapy equipment expected to be worth over €2 billion in 2005, [Ref 5:Pacific Growth Equities], a growth of over 80% from 2002 and a compound annual growth rate, (CAGR) value of 14% , the market is obviously strategically important to Europe. However, all market forecasts predict the European share of this market will fall, [4] by 10% in 2010, predominantly to the Japanese, with the US share remaining at approximately 52%. However, the radiation measurement / dosimetry side of radiotherapy, which is a critical part of the effectiveness of quality assured radiotherapy treatment is an area where SMEs are particularly well suited and can dominate. Our partner PTW are a particularly good example of this. They are a renowned world leader of high quality, high performance dosimetry products and yet are an SME.

The global market for dosimetry is valued at around €300 million, which is relatively modest, [ref 7: Frost & Sullivan]. However, the same survey has predicted that with the growth in IMRT and other conformal radiotherapy treatments, the dosimetry market will grow to €828 million by 2008. The growth in the uptake of IMRT treatments, expands this opportunity for European SMEs still further. There are estimated to be between 5500 and 7500 [ref 4] radiotherapy units in the world which have yet to have IMRT technology applied to them. As calculated in section B3, this represents a total penetrable market potential of €101 million. This market is therefore not only extremely attractive to us and other European SMEs engaged in the dosimetry sector, but is becoming the target of non-European Large Enterprises. This is illustrated by the fact that we know Varian are seeking to develop their own dosimetry products, (project name "dose guided radiotherapy"). If Varian, with their 56% global market share, succeed in this venture then there is the very real probability that the European share of the dosimetry market will fall dramatically. This project aims to develop an innovative, IPR protectable technology to keep European SMEs at the forefront of the radiotherapy dosimetry market. As discussed in section 2, the product will have performance levels, (resolution, response time, accuracy) far superior to any other dosimetry product on the market and will be designed to satisfy the stringent demands of IMRT. At the same time it will be cost competitive, (€30k per dosimeter, excluding interface computer) with other lesser dosimetry systems, further stimulating the

This text was taken from a bid for funding. It's very efficient on space – there are more than 1,600 words on these two pages. Putting that in context, two typical pages might contain 1,000 words. As an evaluator, however, just looking at these pages makes your heart sink. These are from a 66-page document. If you have to wade through 66 pages like this, you will be bored senseless and in no mood to fund the project being described. Compare the above with the next example.

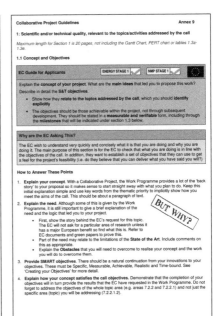

So what is it about this document that makes it easier to read?

1 Fewer words (i.e. more white space)

2 Use of highlighted keywords

3 More headings

4 Bulleted lists

5 Graphics

6 Impact boxes (boxes highlighting key text)

7 Colour (although not too much)[2]

8 Left justification.

Wider margins would also have helped. I'll talk about some of the above list later. However, it is worth saying a a few words about justification.

---

2   I know this book is in black and white but trust me, the page does have subtle colour on and it looks great.

Am I justified in justifying?

Justification means aligning your text with the margins of the page. The text in this book is mainly fully justified. Fully justified text is aligned with both the left and right margins. This is extremely common in column text, such as newspapers and magazines; and in novels. If you look at most fully justified text, you will notice that there are less than ten words to a line. When you have narrow lines and wide margins, full justification can look professional. When you have narrow margins on a piece of A4 paper, full justification limits the white space and makes your writing look very dense.

In circumstances where full justification is unsuitable, use left justification. This is also useful when you have very few words on each line, as full justification messes around with spacing, leaving large ugly gaps. Finally, left justification increases the amount of white space on the page.

Right justified text is not used very often in most documents as it looks messy and unstructured. I can't think of any reason to use it in your writing.

So, a simple rule:

Rule 26: fully justify only if you have around ten to twelve words per line. Otherwise, left justify

HEADINGS

Headings are a crucial part of any document as they provide structure and support to your words. Just as a human without a skeleton would be a blubbery mass, so your document will become unusable without proper support from headings.

- **Make headings big and bold**. They are there to attract the reader's attention, so simply putting the same size text in bold is not enough. Use size and colour to add impact.

- **Make headings meaningful**. Remember that your reader will skim-read. If you give them key facts in headings, you have a greater chance of getting the response you want. For example, you could use **'Results'** as a heading. Alternatively, you could use **'Turnover up 10%'** as a heading. Which will help the skim-reader the most?

- **Number your headings**. If you can grapple with your word processor's outline numbering feature, use it. It allows you to cross-reference, auto-generate a contents table and edit easily, safe in the knowledge that you won't have to keep re-doing your heading numbers.

- **Make your sub-headings clearly different**. In this book, sub-headings aren't numbered and are 13 points smaller than the main first level of headings. This ensures that main headings stand out.

- **Try to start major new sections on a new page**. This does waste space but gives each chapter/section a clear ending and gives the reader a breather. This isn't always possible in all documents but is essential in books and long reports.

- **Attach the heading to the words**. Leave more space above the heading than below, so it doesn't just float around in space.

Last but not least:

Rule 27: use lots of meaningful headings, at least two or three per A4 page

BULLETS

The best way to demonstrate the value of bullets is to use them, so:

- Make sure a bullet only addresses one point.

- Make sure there is space above and below your bulleted list.

- Separate your bullets. This may be by highlighting the key point (see bullets in previous chapter) or by physically spacing them (as here).

- Use numbered lists only if there is a reason for the numbers. For example:

There are three golden rules:

1 Rule 1

2 Rule 2

3 Rule 3.

- Commas, semicolons and nothing at all are all valid ways to end a bullet. Favour commas or nothing for short bullets. For longer bullets, use full stops. In most cases, use a full stop at the end of your last bullet and start a new sentence when you are back into your body text.

- Indent your bullets.

- You may find that bullets look better left-justified, as the indenting reduces the number of words per line, increasing the chances of big gaps in fully justified text.

- Don't make a bulleted list too long, especially if it goes over a couple of pages. This one is already a bit long but I'm using it for effect (honest!).

TABLES AND DIAGRAMS

Sometimes, information can be more easily digested if it is presented graphically. Remember our aim with any document is to make it persuasive and, if a table or diagram helps the reader, it improves the odds of getting what you want. A note of caution, however: bad diagrams do more harm than bad text.

Turning the tables on excess words

Generally, lists and data can be represented in tables. Take this example of repetitious phrases to avoid:

Join together	Revert back
Sneak quietly	Merge together
Sink down	Past experience
Repeat again	Fundamentally basic

This could have been presented in a list. Instead, columns were used. This is effectively a table without the lines. This helps add a visual change to the text, as well as being more efficient on space. Data are even easier to tabulate. For example:

The Northern branch turned over £23K in July, £24K in August and £28K in September. By comparison, the Southern branch only managed £22K, £23K and £25K in the same period.

This would be much better shown as:

Month	Northern branch	Southern branch
July	£23,000	£22,000
August	£24,000	£23,000
September	£28,000	£25,000

Some points to note about tables:

- Sans serif fonts are good for presenting data.
- Right justify numbers – it's easier to compare them.
- Make your header row stand out.
- Provide a numbered caption for your table. Most word processors can outline number tables for you, helping with editing and cross-referencing.

Do pictures speak a thousand words?

Yes and no. For some, a film can never compare with really good descriptive writing. Why? Because a book relies on the reader's imagination to create a vision of the world. This is very personal and thus more appealing to a specific reader. Conversely, a film is one person's vision of that world. Only rarely does anyone say "I liked the book but the film was better".

That said, some things are extremely difficult to express in writing. An expression on an old man's face could take an entire chapter to explain; or a single picture to show. Companies also invest millions in logos and visual branding as it can often say more about the company than any slogan.

Graphics are particularly useful in business writing. Wherever possible, use them to show data, diagrams, prototypes, logos, etc. Flowcharts and labelled examples can also work very well.

The following rules apply:

- label your diagrams clearly;
- leave plenty of white space around them;
- position them as close as possible to the text discussing them and always on the same page;
- introduce the diagram, show it, and then discuss it.

SUMMARY

Presentation makes your document more accessible and more impressive so don't ignore it.

- Select a **font** that is easy to read and suitable for your audience.

- Favour serif fonts for body text and sans serif for impact.

- Use an uncluttered **layout** that maximises white space.

- Make use of **tables, diagrams and bullets** to break up body text and give your writing more variation and impact.

10

Tips for Common Documents

Whilst everything in this book applies to all types of document, some have specific features worthy of further attention. A great many books and websites will give you tips on writing the best CV, executive summary, research proposal, etc. and I'm keen not to repeat this content or fill up the section with obvious statements. Therefore, this section is my take on these common documents. Although some of the advice can be found elsewhere, hopefully some insights will be new to you.

In this section, we will look at:

- emails
- writing for the web
- the CV/resume
- executive summaries
- grant funding.

MORE EFFECTIVE EMAILS

The vast majority of documents you will ever create will be emails. However, most people put significantly less effort into writing them than they do into all other documents. The result is that email content (meaning and tone) is correctly interpreted in as little as 50 per cent of cases.

Just being aware of this fact could save you serious problems. To help further, I've included my top 11[1] tips for effective emails below:

1   **Use an informative subject line.** People with very active inboxes often need to prioritise their email reading. Help them do it by telling them what your email is about. Writing URGENT in your subject line doesn't help if everyone considers

---

1   I had a nice round top 10 until one of my proofreaders suggested another. He was right though.

their email to be urgent. Let your reader decide their priorities. Also, emails will often be retrieved at a later date for replies or cross-referencing. A relevant subject line will really help.

2 **Give your email one main point.** Also, make sure it has no more than one requested action. Your reader will skim-read the email and will usually only have the time to absorb one issue. If this one point is clearly communicated, with an associated action, there is more chance of this action happening. This ties in with point 1 above – if your subject line refers to one point but the body text refers to three, the other two will be lost the moment that email is closed.

3 **Include context.** Don't assume your reader will remember the details of the email they sent you. If necessary, include their email or excerpts from it. At the very least, write in full sentences explaining your response.

4 **An email is a document.** All the rules in this book apply to emails as well as to more formal documents. Use 'Reader Response = Result', follow formatting rules and edit at least once.

5 **Don't write as you talk.** This may seem odd given previous chapters. However, most of the misinformation transmitted through email is down to people writing *exactly* as they talk. The reason is **tone**. In face-to-face and phone conversations, a significant amount of the information is transmitted by tone of voice. This is lost in email and can lead to misinterpretation. Consider the sentence:

"I'd choose Dave, maybe Steve as well. The last person I'd pick would be Chris."

Does it mean I'd choose three people or does it mean I'd choose two and would never dream of choosing Chris? In conversation, intonation would make this very clear (try it).

Always remind yourself that the only information your reader has to go on is contained in the words. You should always ...

6 **Assume your tone will be misinterpreted.** In casual emails, texts and instant messaging, people use emoticons[2] to express emotion. In a business email, we don't have that luxury so have to be very careful to make sure the reader understands our meaning. When you proofread your email, look for any possible double meanings and assume the worst. Re-write to make it clear exactly what you mean. The above example could be rewritten as:

"I'd choose Dave, Steve and Chris, in that order."

7 **Be polite.** One sure-fire way to avoid the tone issue is to be polite. If your reader doesn't know you, they will form an image of you from your writing. If you are polite from the start, they will tend to read the rest of the email assuming it is from a polite person and will give you the benefit of the doubt. If you are abrupt, the reader will tend to put a negative spin on any areas of ambiguity.

8 **Be concise but conversational.** Email is a strange animal as it is neither a pure letter, nor a verbal conversation. Conciseness is good but too much will be seen as abrupt and rude. Conversely, conversational excess words will help build a tone but too much will hide the message. Consider these three examples:

"Hi Dave, hope you are keeping well, um, I was just wondering if you wouldn't mind sending across the weekly figures 'cause I've got the management conference on Tuesday and I really need to get the consolidated numbers done today. Before 4:00 would be great but don't worry if it's after, I'll be here late."

---

2 Combinations of punctuation marks, designed to look like smiley (or sad) faces, such as :-) ;-) and :-(.

This is something you would most likely leave on an answer phone. Written down, it is long, cluttered and inefficient. A more concise version would be:

"Dave, please send the weekly figures by 4:00."

This may be fine for some relationships but could also be seen as quite cold and unfriendly. Something in the middle is probably best:

"Hi Dave, could you send me over the weekly figures please? If you could get them to me by 4:00, that would be great."

9 **Assume others will read your email.** In some companies, all emails are open to being checked by management. Even if this isn't the case, email is a permanent, legally admissible record that is easy to distribute. Do not write anything that you would not be happy about others seeing. Also, you always risk accidentally sending emails to the wrong people. Before sending, always stop and check your recipients. Even better, set up a rule in your email that delays sending your emails for a couple of minutes. This has saved my skin a few times!

10 **Why are you sending an email?** Only email if you have to. A phone call is more personal, helps build relationships and is less likely to be misinterpreted. Reply only to those who need to know and don't send a message that has no value for the reader. For example, if you receive a group message asking where the stapler has gone, don't reply to all saying "I don't know". Remember, this is a document as well as a conversation so must have a purpose.

11 **Don't send an email when emotional.** Unlike a letter, an email can be sent in seconds. Once it has gone, you have to live with the consequences. If you are feeling angry or upset, write the email and then sleep on it. In the morning, re-read the message. If you still agree with it, send it. If not, delete it and start again.

WRITING FOR THE WEB

Perhaps surprisingly, this will be a very short section. Why? Because the key principle in writing for the web is conciseness. I've read through around 30 lists of 'top 10 web writing tips' and all the advice is covered in earlier chapters. However, just so you don't feel short-changed, here are a few extra tips when creating web content:

1 **What is the website for?** It is crucial you understand the purpose of the site. Many companies assume they have to have a website but don't put any thought into why. Until you understand why you want a website, you can't possibly write something to do the job.

2 **Give the reader some reward.** Most of the time, a reader will only go to a website if there is something in it for them. Give them titbits of information they can use, or at least something to hold their interest (such as case studies). You could even include software tools to help them choose the right product.

3 **Make pages the right length.** Some websites become obsessed with page length, limiting text to one screen only. Others will dump everything into one massive page ten screens long. Think about what you are prepared to read through. For example, the BBC website tends to have pages between two and five screens long, although it has very wide margins. With narrower margins, you may want to be at the lower end of that range.

4 **Skim-reading is even more common on the web.** Most of the time a business website is not an end in itself, unless it is for an online retailer. As a result, people will tend to skim through looking for the pieces of information of most value. Rarely will anyone settle down in a comfy chair with a mug of cocoa to read a website. Use lots of informative sub-headings, impact boxes and highlighting to draw the reader to the key points.

5 **Make it easy for people to contact you.** Linked to point 4, the

most common reason for someone to visit a website is to find out about your company. Hopefully, once they see how great you are, they'll want to contact you, so make it easy for them. Wherever possible, give named contacts – be people rather than a faceless company. Likewise, give direct email addresses and telephone numbers if you can. At the very least, provide relevant-sounding email addresses (sales@acecorp.com, service@ acecorp.com), even if they all end up in the same inbox.

6 **Draw out your site map.** If you can't fit it on to a sheet of A4 paper, think again. Don't make the content so fragmented that the site map looks like an electrician's nightmare. If you can fit all the information a reader wants on to one page (accommodating tip 3 above), do so.

7 **Web design and content creation are not the same thing.** Some people are expert writers, some people are expert web designers. Do not assume that, if you are one of these, you are automatically the other.

8 **Don't forget about the rest of this book.** As I said before, web writing is simply good, concise writing. Understand your audience, why you are writing and be persuasive.

PERSUASIVE CVs

Regardless of your job, almost everyone will need to write an effective CV at some point. In fact, persuasive writing doesn't get much more critical than this; after all, your livelihood depends on it. As mentioned in the introduction, I'm not going to repeat all the sound advice in other CV-writing guides. Instead, here are my top tips, from both sides of the recruitment table.

Understand the point of a CV

A strange heading, I know. However, as discussed earlier, you have to know the result you want in order to write persuasively. In this case, the result is to move to the next stage of the recruitment process, usually the interview. This means you don't have to convince the recruiter you are the best person for the job; you have to convince them you are *potentially* the best person for the job. This actually takes a bit of pressure off: you don't need to be perfect, just interesting. This leads on to another point:

Don't include the detail on everything

First, this fills up valuable space: a good CV should never be more than three pages long and ideally it should be two pages. Secondly, if there's nothing the recruiter needs to know about you, why would they want to interview you? It forces them to make a decision based solely on your CV, which means it must be perfect. Finally, leaving out some detail leads the recruiter to ask the questions you want. For example, if you mention a major marketing project for Volvic mineral water, but don't go into detail, your recruiter will almost certainly mark up your CV with a note to ask about this at interview. It's much better to spend the interview talking about your triumphs than answering the standard questions. Remember to strike a balance though: too little detail and it looks like you haven't done anything worth mentioning.

Personalise to the job

Don't write one generic CV and rely on your cover letter to explain how this fits the job in question. Instead, tailor the CV to suit. This may involve re-ordering the information, emphasising certain skills from different jobs, or even 'dumbing down' your achievements (you can be over-qualified as well as under-qualified).

Exploit the cover letter

If you are able to include a cover letter, make the most of it. Keep it to one side of A4 if you can, but apply everything you know about persuasion to it. If you can write an excellent cover letter that establishes the correct emotive response, you will bias the way the recruiter reads the actual CV. Where the CV is a fixed, factual template, this may be the only chance you have to emotionally influence the recruiter.

Avoid clichés

Unless you are applying for a job with a start-up company, odds are your recruiter has seen hundreds, if not thousands, of CVs. They will not be impressed by stock phrases such as:

- "I enjoy working on my own or as part of a team."
- "I am hard-working, dedicated and prepared to go the extra mile."
- "I am reliable and honest."
- "I am self-motivating."
- "My hobbies include reading and going out."

Rather than include vague, general statements like the ones above, use the space to talk about how a particular example of your work demonstrates the trait in question.

Don't write in the third person

"David is a hard-working and talented individual."

Don't do it, it just sounds weird.

Presentation is king

A CV is as much a visual document as a written one. In 2010, an average of 70 graduates applied for every graduate position available. If your CV is one of those 70, how will you ensure you get noticed? Most CVs are fairly unexciting so you don't have to do much to be noticed; just make sure you keep it classy. Simple borders, impact boxes, subtle colour and careful font selection can all make your CV stand out for the right reasons. Don't be tempted to show off your Photoshop skills or some cool 3-D text effect you've discovered in Word.

Try disarming honesty

Experienced recruiters have extremely sensitive bullsh*t meters. If you worked as a server in Burger King, don't write something like this:

"2004–2006 – Senior Customer Service Representative.
During this period I was retained by a major food manufacturer and retailer. My role was to ensure customer needs were met throughout the procurement process. The challenging role required strong customer service skills, coupled with accountancy, health and safety monitoring and ensuring optimal hygiene levels."

If you genuinely have the skills needed for the job, don't be afraid of talking about your past roles, warts and all. It is a real breath of fresh air for a recruiter to see someone prepared to tell it like it is, which can be a great psychological advantage. For example, you could try something like this:

"2004–2006 – Food Server, Burger King.
Although this could be considered the low-point of my CV, this job taught me more valuable skills than you might think. I needed to remain positive and efficient through many hours of mind-numbing tedium; I had to remain calm when dealing with extremely difficult customers; and I had to gel with a constantly changing team with a wide range of abilities and personalities. Whilst not advancing my technical skills, I honestly feel this job has prepared me for any other challenge I may face in my working life."

By accepting your experience for what it is, but still finding positives, you will catch the recruiter off-guard and possibly even make them smile. If you can back that up with genuinely relevant skills you'll be ahead of 90 per cent of the other applicants.

EXECUTIVE SUMMARIES AND ABSTRACTS

The phrase 'executive summary' deserves a little attention, as it tells us much about what it is and isn't. The executive summary is designed to be read by busy executives who don't have time to read the whole document. Executives are the decision-makers, i.e. the people you need to persuade. If an executive decision can be made on the strength of the summary, the rest of the document is largely irrelevant, provided it doesn't contradict the summary. If the reader doesn't like what you've said, they won't read on. If the reader likes what you've said, they will read on only to confirm their already formed opinion (confirmation bias).

In other words, **the executive summary is your document**. Everything else simply provides the detail you can't fit into the summary.

Most people approach the executive summary last and simply cut-and-paste text from the document to build a shortened version, often at the last minute. I propose a different approach – do your executive summary first.

This may seem strange but stick with me. Using the concise writing techniques promoted in this book, you should be producing bullet-point plans mapping out your story and main arguments. Fill in the bare minimum details and you have an executive summary. Fill in greater detail and supporting evidence and you have the document. Clearly you will need to polish the summary once your body text has evolved but there is no logical reason to leave it to the end, when you run the risk of rushing to hit the deadline. Remember, **the executive summary is your document**.

So what should the summary look like and how long should it be? The length really depends on the total document size but, considering most business books can be condensed to five A4 pages or less,[3] there is no reason why an executive summary should be more than three pages.

The structure of the summary or abstract should mirror your document structure, as it is based on the same story. It should always include:

- the reason a decision needs to be made;
- the decision you want them to make;

---

3 If you don't believe me, try it.

■ the reasons why they should choose the option you want them to.

For offer-based documents, such as bids, tenders and proposals, the following formats are useful options:

■ Create empathy with the client and their requirements.

■ Outline the characteristics of a successful solution/supplier.

■ Provide an overview of your offer, in line with the above.

■ Why you? Why not the Competition? Differentiate yourself.

■ **Situation** – Why are we where we are?

■ **Opportunity** – What can be changed/improved?

■ **Solution** – What do we offer to exploit this opportunity?

■ **Approach** – How will we achieve this?

■ **Impact** – How will this help?

The persuasive writing example shown in Chapter 2 is a typical story-based abstract.

GRANT FUNDING

Tens of thousands of requests for grants are written every year in the UK, yet only a tiny percentage are successful. The applicant understands precisely why the funding is needed and is often completely at a loss as to why the funding body doesn't agree. Obviously, the reason you want the funding is a major part of any application: ask for a grant to set up a vivisection theme park and no amount of effective writing is going to help. However, the most common reason for good ideas failing to get funding is poor writing. The following tips and tricks should help you eliminate the most common errors:

Who's paying and who's reviewing?

For most business decisions, the person making the decision has a direct financial interest in its success. For example, a manager who blows the departmental budget on a bad consultant will have to answer to someone. This is not always the case with grant funding. A typical example is research funding. The European Commission (EC) runs a huge programme to part-fund companies with innovative technology ideas. The EC has set aside the cash but doesn't decide who gets it. That job is left up to independent reviewers, the nature of whom varies from call to call. In the general calls, it could be academics, consultants, researchers or businessmen and there will always be at least three people examining your proposal.

Although the marking scheme is laid down by the EC, the more subtle persuasive factors are very different when it's not your money. For example, if it were your money, you would be most interested in things like cost, payback period, return on investment, market size, intellectual property and exploitation rights. When it is not your money, you are more interested in being engaged, entertained and excited. It doesn't matter how good your idea is, if the evaluator is bored after the first few pages, they are likely to turn it down. Some of the tips below will help you achieve this balance between facts and entertainment.

Storytelling and logic trains

Storytelling becomes essential in grant applications for two main reasons:

1 it helps to provide a logical structure;
2 it engages the reader.

I would strongly recommend using a 'logic train'. This is

a story structure that presents the critical facts in a logical order, meaning it should be difficult for an evaluator to disagree with the reasons for your application. It is also an engaging story, helping to draw the reader in and keeping their interest. At the logic train's core is a 'problem/opportunity to solution' structure with some additional flourishes. In particular, it is designed to respond to the evaluator's thoughts as soon as they come into their mind. It is structured as follows:

1 There is a problem/opportunity:

Oh that's terrible/fantastic, we should do something.

2 It is big enough to justify the grant funding requested:

Surely someone has done something about this?

3 No one else has come up with an adequate solution:

Damn, that's a shame.

4 We have an idea for that solution:

Hoorah, off you go then.

5 We can't just do it because there are the following barriers:

Damn, that's a shame.

6 Grant funding can overcome these barriers in the following specific ways:

Oh, that's handy, I'd like to help.

7 If we overcome the barriers and develop the solution, the benefits will be significant (for everyone the grant programme is looking to help):

Right, we'd better give you some money then.

I also term this the 'Boo-Hooray' story. You present related bad news and good news alternately, building towards the final good news. By doing this, you show the evaluator you've covered all the angles and thought of all major objections and barriers to your initiative.

Depending on the need for evidence and the scale of the application, this logic train can be between half a page and two pages long. The logic train approach also makes a nice abstract/executive summary format for grant applications.

Over the years I've seen several hundred grant applications. I would say around 80 per cent of proposals with good logic trains get funded, versus 20 per cent with poor logic trains. Invest as much time and effort as you can in creating your story. Then, spend even more time trying to break it.

Remember, if your evaluator is not spending their own money, they will be more interested in the story than the minutiae of the financial details. Tell a good story, stir up emotions and create a desire to help and the combination of primacy effects and confirmation bias will have half your battle won.

Analogous reversal

Although the evaluator of your bid is not always spending their own money, often they are. Even when they are not, a good evaluator will still be looking to spend that money wisely. It is often difficult to imagine yourself in the role of an evaluator, especially when it comes to your own bid ("of course I'd fund it, it's brilliant!"). However, if you use an analogous situation and reverse the roles (hence the name), you will find it fairly easy to ask the right questions and hence plan in advance for them.

To explain this more clearly, let's use an example. Suppose I am bidding for a grant for developing a new product or technology. I need to put myself in the shoes of someone making a product-buying decision on behalf of someone else. A good two-part analogy would be:

Part 1: Your elderly neighbour would like to improve their heating system and a salesman from a solar thermal heating company is coming round. Your neighbour has asked you to sit in on the sales meeting to make sure they aren't deceived by the salesman. What questions would you ask the seller before you would let your neighbour part with any cash?

The questions you would ask might include:

- Why do I need one?
- What is it?
- How does it work?
- How much will it cost?
- What are the benefits?
- Does this represent value for money?
- Can I get the same thing cheaper elsewhere?
- What happens if I wait a few years?
- What are the alternatives?
- What work needs doing?
- What exactly am I getting for my money?
- How long will it take?
- Will you be doing all the work yourself?
- Can I see references or testimonials?
- Can I have an itemised quote?
- Is the work guaranteed?
- Will my insurers cover this if it goes wrong?

Part 2: The salesman reveals his company is looking to expand and is seeking investment. He asks if you would be interested in investing. What questions would you ask before committing to invest?

This time the questions might include:

- What is your current turnover and balance sheet?
- Is there a market? How big is it?
- What's my financial return on investment?
- What do I get to own as an investor?
- What's your five-year strategy?
- How secure is my investment?
- Who else is investing?

You will find the answers to these questions are exactly what any evaluator wants to hear before awarding a grant, loan or investment for a new product. A similar analogous reversal can be created for services, charitable work or other types of grant. Don't rely on the list above – work out your own analogy and questions. Ideally, get two or three other people to do the same exercise until you have a comprehensive list of general questions. Once you do, apply them to your own bid and make sure you have answered them all.

By putting yourself in a similar situation, you can see the evaluator's point of view while remaining detached from the emotive issues linked to your own application. On this note, make sure you choose an example from which you can remain emotionally detached. If you are a firm believer that every home should have solar thermal heating, you will miss questions you should be asking.

Show your workings

This is an example of the Power of Because. If you present information without providing evidence, you can be sure the evaluator will look into it. However, if you provide evidence, chances are the evaluator won't check it. I have seen many a good proposal fail because evidence was missing, despite the claim being true. Conversely, I've seen many proposals with terrible calculation errors get funded because the workings have been shown and the evaluator hasn't bothered to check them. What this boils down to is:

Show how you have arrived at your conclusion by showing calculations, references or educated opinion. However, don't spend too long justifying yourself; if there is a plausible 'because', the evaluator will usually be happy.

Beware the web

Ten years ago, if you wanted to find anything out, you had to work hard. Information was as valuable as knowledge on how to apply it. The advent of the internet changed this. Now, information is just a few mouse-clicks away. This has changed grant applications considerably. The first thing any evaluator does now is hit the web to check out you and your claims. There are three major pitfalls:

1 **Your web presence.** In your application, you will undoubtedly make yourself sound fantastic. If the evaluator looks you up on the web, will they see the same picture? Type your company name into Google. Does your website come top of the list? Are there review sites with bad opinions of you on the first few pages of results? Are there recent press releases? Does your website look like it belongs to a serious, professional organisation? Do you even have a website? Make sure you polish your web presence to match the image you want the evaluators to see.

2 **Your bid subject.** This crops up a lot in research bids. Companies looking for venture capital need to be seen as close to market. For research funding, you need to be much further away. If your website promotes one image, and your bid another, you

could risk upsetting the evaluator. Make sure the evaluator will not get to see anything that contradicts your application.

3 **Your competitors.** In most technology grant applications, you will need to rubbish your competitors in order to justify why your new approach is better. If the evaluator finds something you haven't talked about that looks just as good, your bid has just died. Search the first ten pages of Google and other popular search engines, using a variety of keywords, to find any serious competitors to your approach. Make sure all of these are discussed and dismissed (for good reason) in your proposal. Also, remember the evaluator will usually be looking at sales literature. Make sure you explain clearly why these approaches are inferior to counteract the very positive image the evaluator might see.

If it's too good to be true, it probably is

This one hurts. Trust me, I know. You can have the best grant application ever. What you are proposing is completely revolutionary and will make billions for your company and the funding organisation. The evaluators don't believe you and don't award the grant. This has happened to me on a research project. We demonstrated a tenfold improvement over the existing approach. The evaluators didn't believe it. We resubmitted with a four times improvement. This time they believed it. We actually had to undersell the technology to make it convincing.

Again, analogous reversal is useful to see if your claims will be believed. If someone tried to sell you a product claiming it was ten times better than the rivals, you'd be suspicious. If you do make big claims, make sure the evidence is rock-solid and give the evidence before the big claim. If the evaluator works it out for themselves before you tell them, they are more likely to accept it. Finally, consider downgrading your claims if you are still worried. If the evaluator ends up thinking "hey, this could be even better than they're claiming", it can actually be a positive for the project. Just make sure you strike the balance between fundable advance and outrageous claim.

FEEDBACK, FEAR AND A FAVOUR

Although this is mostly related to editing, it seems appropriate to talk about feedback at the end.

Many people are afraid of having their work critiqued. One writer I work with said they were more nervous before one of my evaluations than before their driving test.

But criticism and comment are essential. I'm a professional evaluator and editor and I still have to force myself to seek criticism. However, it is important you get the right people to comment on your work. The most important reviewers are your audience or people like them. Without this feedback, you will never know whether your approach works or why it is failing. When seeking comment:

- Keep the number of reviewers appropriate to the document. If you ask ten people, you will get ten different sets of comments, many of them contradictory. I'd suggest using between two and four reviewers, depending on the importance of the document.

- Try to vary the type of reviewer. If you have four, make two representative of your audience, make one a relevant expert and one a person with no knowledge of your area (e.g. a family member or non-work friend).

- Ask for explanation and suggestion with the comments – don't let people get away with saying "I don't like it".

- Consider asking different reviewers to look at different aspects of the document. For example, one may look at presentation whilst another looks at content.

- If it is appropriate to get feedback from your final audience, do so. Although feedback can't help on the current document, it is invaluable for improving your future work.

- Finally, don't take it to heart. The comments are on your document, not you. We never stop learning and, sometimes, you won't know what your target audience really wants until you see their feedback.

And now, the favour

I need feedback as much as anyone else so please take the time to review this book. This could be some comments sent back to me direct, an email to my publisher or a review on a website such as Amazon. If you want to make the task more interesting, set yourself a word limit (I'd suggest fewer than 100 words). Any comments, good or bad, will be gratefully received. After all, I'm not writing this book for me.

SUMMARY

Whilst the techniques presented in this book are suitable for any document, it's worth knowing some specific techniques for common document types:

- **Emails** – treat them like any other written document and make the point of the email obvious.

- **Writing for the web** – keep it concise.

- **CVs** – customise, consider presentation and be honest.

- **Executive summary** – it is the document.

- **Grant funding** – use a logic train to tell a good story.
- **Feedback** – it's a good thing, so embrace it.

11

Persuasion – the Dark Arts

I recently read *The Duck that Won the Lottery* by Julian Baggini. This contains 100 'bad' arguments, i.e. arguments with a fundamental flaw. Whilst there's no doubting all these arguments are flawed, some are still very persuasive if your reader doesn't spot the fallacy at the heart of the argument.

This presents me with a moral dilemma – should I advocate the use of lies and deceit as a persuasive tool? Actually it isn't much of a dilemma as these flawed arguments are used every day anyway, especially in politics and journalism. If you're going to do it, you might as well understand what you are doing. This chapter pulls together a selection of interesting fallacious arguments from various sources and gives you some guidance on how to use them and, implicitly, how to spot them when used against you.

However, before going into detail, I want to include a couple of caveats:

1 **Understand the risks.** The problem with using a fallacious argument is that your reader may spot it. No one likes to be deceived so, if they do spot it, you will likely do more harm than good. Far better to use a properly reasoned argument if you possibly can.

2 **Understand the consequences.** Your primary objective in writing will be to persuade someone to do something. However, this will rarely be your only objective. For example, you will usually want to keep your reader happy and maintain a long-term relationship with them. Therefore, deceiving or threatening your reader may get you a short-term win but could seriously damage your future relationship.

So, these are last-resort tactics when normal persuasive methods won't work. Use them sparingly and understand the risks and consequences. Take a deep breath, hold your nose and let's delve into the murky depths of persuasion to investigate the dark arts.

ASSUME CAUSALITY

Sometimes you want to convince a reader that something works when it really doesn't. This is seen regularly in the world of complementary medicine.

I want to sell a revolutionary new medical treatment that realigns your Chi by getting ants to carry tiny magnets across your body. I claim it can cure bad backs, depression and the common cold. At first glance, this seems an impossible task. However, with assumed causality, I'll be selling the treatment in no time. The three main weapons I have at my disposal are:

1 **It's no coincidence.** I can give people ant therapy and some of them will feel better afterwards. Most of this group will assume it is the ant therapy working, even though it is most likely just the attention, regression to the mean or placebo (see Ben Goldacre's book *Bad Science* for more on this). But people like cause and effect so some will swear it worked. I now have my social proof and examples saying "the patient was ill, they had ant therapy and got better. It's no coincidence". In business, people use this all the time to claim credit for success. If you put in a little bit of input on projects once you know they will be a success, you can claim it's no coincidence everything you worked on was successful.

2 **There's so much evidence.** Repeat the above hundreds of times and you have 'overwhelming proof' ant therapy is the latest miracle cure. It doesn't matter that it's all circumstantial evidence; you keep bombarding the reader with enough of it and, sooner or later, they'll start to think there must be something in it.

3 **How else would you explain it?** Of course, some unhelpful individual might start to question the way ant therapy works. In which case, you can always fall back on this argument. No

matter how ridiculous your theory is, it will often be accepted if no one can come up with a better one. Challenge them to; when they can't, you can claim this validates your theory.

Just to reiterate, these arguments have more holes than Swiss cheese but they've still been effective enough to help establish multi-million pound markets for some complementary therapies in the UK.

IT'S COMMON SENSE, STUPID

Everyone likes to think they have common sense or great intuition. It's true everyone does possess common sense; it's just that it isn't always a good thing to have. If I won the lottery two weeks in a row with the same numbers, most people would assume I was cheating. However, if Sarah Jones in Redruth won one week with one set of numbers, then Steven Hughes in Aberdeen the next with another set, no one would bat an eyelid. However, both situations are equally likely (see 'Abuse statistics' below).

Yet common sense is still prized and calling someone's intuition into question can be quite insulting. As such, people will tend to shy away from questioning something if you say it is common sense. After all, if they question your point, aren't they showing they don't have common sense?

So how do you use this in practice? Here's an example:

We should pay an incentive bonus for staff in attendance on Mondays and Fridays. Obviously, this is when most staff will be tempted to 'throw a sickie' in order to take a long weekend. An attendance bonus will reduce absences and increase productivity.

According to the UK Office for National Statistics, weekday absence rates are pretty much equal, with Monday the least likely day for absences. The 'common sense' of Monday and Friday sick leave just doesn't hold true across all industries, ages and regions. However, if you are a union lobbying for more pay for staff, an argument such as this may be very effective in increasing pay while seemingly benefiting the employers more.

Even if something isn't common sense, claiming it is can be enough. Just don't try to be too ambitious: although it's common sense to use bicycle couriers in inner-city London, don't claim they're the obvious choice for international freight.

IT'S COMMON KNOWLEDGE

It's amazing what you can get away with if you over-generalise. A quick search of this book reveals I have claimed something is 'always' the case at least five times but I doubt anyone has noticed (until now, obviously).

If you do not have the evidence to back up a claim, you can always try to generalise. The following phrases (or variants) are often used:

- "It is generally accepted that …"
- "The widely held/discredited view is …"
- "It is believed that …"
- "Always/never"
- "Everyone/no one"
- "The traditional view has been … However, it is now thought …"
- "The majority of people/businesses/managers …"

Of course, your reader may know you are completely wrong in your claim so be careful where you use generalisations. However, a few sprinkled here and there can get you out of a sticky situation without your reader noticing. In fact, it may even lead them to believe your claim as they subconsciously stash it away as fact.

ABUSE STATISTICS

The staple diet of journalists and politicians, dodgy statistics have contributed to health scares, wrongful convictions and even wars. Here are four of the most common ways of twisting numbers to suit your needs:

1 **Ignore the base rate.** I have software that can correctly spot a credit card fraud 90% of the time and calls a good transaction a fraud just 0.1% of the time (false positive rate). This seems pretty good on the surface. However, if the rate at which frauds occur (the base rate) is taken into account, is it still as good? If there is 1 fraud in every 1,000 transactions and I look at 100,000 examples, I should spot 90 of the 100 frauds. However, 1 in every 1,000 genuine transactions will be flagged up as a fraud when it isn't. This means, of the frauds I detect, 90 will be genuine and about 100 will be false positives. This would probably be acceptable for the industry. However, if 1 fraud occurs in every 10,000 transactions, the situation gets worse. Now, I still have around 100 false positives but only 9 genuine frauds. This would be disastrous for the industry, as the money saved in preventing fraud would be swallowed up handling all the customer complaints from false positives. If you want poor statistical data to look good, ignore the base rate and just claim the percentages.

2 **Compare best and worst cases.** Let's say you are comparing your product with that of a rival. On average, your product is worse. Never fear, simply compare the incomparable. For example, on a car, you could compare your predicted or laboratory fuel consumption with a rival's actual average from

real-world driving. Alternatively, you could compare their average to your extra-urban cycle, claiming your car could achieve 'up to 30% higher fuel consumption' than your rival. Note the use of the words 'up to'. These have been responsible for more dodgy advertising claims than any other phrase. Without the details in place, your reader won't be able to make an informed judgement and is more likely to simply accept your assertions.

3 **Selection bias.** This states that the results of any statistical analysis are heavily influenced by the source of your data. Take cosmetics for example. Almost every ad says something like "9 out of 10 women agree it gave them younger-looking skin". So where do they get their numbers from? If it were me, I'd send free samples of the product to around 150 regular users of my brand and ask them to rate it. Not only do these people like my company already, they now feel obligated to be nice as I've given them free stuff. Secondly, I'd word the questionnaire to increase the likelihood of the user being positive, by using false dichotomies (see 'And a few more' later in this chapter). If I didn't get the results I wanted, I would do another survey. Of course, I wouldn't ever claim 100% satisfaction, as that might look contrived. Better to go with 77% or 86%. In fact, as an aside, a very unscientific search of Google shows most face creams to be between 75% and 90% effective.[1] The same approach can be applied to any other set of statistics – by cherry-picking your data and leaving out the detail, you can achieve the most persuasive numbers.

4 **Find patterns in randomness.** This links back to causality. If you can find a cluster of random events, you can claim they aren't random but indicative of something else entirely. The book

---

1 I spotted this in my proofread. The creams aren't shown to be effective; the stats just show 77% of women in a contrived sample agree with a statement. I've done exactly what the ads want me to do, which is assume anecdotal survey results equals proof of effectiveness.

The Bible Code worked entirely on this principle. Worse, there have been several miscarriages of justice based almost solely on such dodgy statistics (in particular the case of Sally Clarke). In using this approach, you are asking the question "how likely is it to happen by chance?", knowing the reader will say "very unlikely" in reply.

To illustrate this point, I'm going to prove my staff are faking their sick days. Let's say we have 15 people in the office. Bill and Sarah were both 'off sick' last Friday, but no one else was ill. As my staff are pretty healthy and only take one sick day a year on average, I'm sure they're skiving off together. After all, what are the odds of that happening by chance?

There are 220 working days a year. To prove my point, I can say there is a 1 in 220 chance Bill was off sick on Friday. The odds of Sarah being off sick at exactly the same time are 1 in 220 times 1 in 220, or 1 in 48,400. Time to start the disciplinary proceedings.

Or is it? What I've done here is assume Bill and Sarah were both off on one particular day, which would indeed be unlikely. However, it could have been any two staff off together on any working day in the year. In fact, there are 105 different pairs of staff that could be off together on any given day. Although the likelihood of each pair being off on a particular day is small, there are so many possible times for a pair to be off, it soon becomes quite likely one combination will happen. In this case, the likelihood of a pair of colleagues being off together at some point in the year is 38%. Although the data are entirely random, I've spotted a pattern that seems unlikely so have assumed it couldn't be chance. This is another example of the failure of common sense. However, even though I'd be wrong, most people would believe my reasoning and statistics and agree my staff were up to no good.

In short, if you see a pattern in random data, you can claim it is significant by ignoring the fact it probably turned up by chance and asking the rhetorical question "what are the odds that this could happen by chance?" Throw in some dodgy statistics proving your point and you may just show the highly probable is almost impossible.

WIDEN OR NARROW DEFINITIONS

Wouldn't it be nice to claim you were the best at something? However, not everyone can be the best. If you're not, why not change the meaning of 'best'? You can do this by widening or narrowing the definitions you use.

For example, perhaps you want to claim you have more customers than any other firm in the same industry. If you don't, try changing the definition of 'customer'. You could widen it to include quotes issued and not just work completed. Alternatively you could narrow the definition to exclude numbers that don't help your cause. Your new definition of 'customer' could be only those you have a long-term relationship with or who spend over a certain amount. Again, this trick is used by journalists to create sensational headlines. A city can be called the most violent in Britain on the basis of all crime, all violent crime, all gun crime, all murders, all deaths or even all gun-related murders. By tailoring your definition, you can legitimately make bold headline claims that draw your reader in.

FLATTERY WILL GET YOU EVERYWHERE

As a general rule, people have a higher opinion of themselves than is actually warranted. For example:

- between 70% and 90% of people think they are better drivers than average
- 87% of MBA students in a study rated their academic ability above average
- people of lower skill are more likely to over-estimate their ability.

This information is far more important than reality – as far as our reader is concerned, this is reality. Two particular biases make the situation worse. First, confirmation bias (see Chapter 3) ensures your reader will ignore anything that disproves their ability/intelligence. Secondly, attributional bias will reinforce their belief in their own superiority. Attributional bias means we attribute our successes to skill and our failures to bad luck. Likewise, we attribute others' success to luck and their failures to their lack of ability. Along with others, these biases ensure the majority of us have an overly inflated opinion of ourselves.

Rather than battle this, we can improve our chances of persuading a reader by agreeing with how great they are. Consider using some or all of the following forms of flattery:

- We trust you to make the right decision.
- We remember exactly who you are.
- We wouldn't exist without you.
- We have special options for people of your ability.

■ We need your help because you're the best.

■ As you clearly understand this, we'll just give you the outline.

Some of these are more than just bare-faced flattery. Special options can cost more, for example. My nephew was told he was too good for the cheaper group guitar lessons and so needed more expensive one-on-one tuition. No parent would wish to deny their child that sort of opportunity if they could afford it, so the guitar tutor makes more money. I'm sure my nephew really does need extra tuition but, if I were a hard-up guitar tutor with low moral standards, I'd do something similar.

The only thing to watch with flattery is that you don't go too far. Words like sycophantic, toadying and brown-nosing are not compliments. Also, flattery works best if your reader has a high ego. Those with low self-esteem can be made to feel good but you run the risk of their viewing your efforts more suspiciously. As always, know your reader.

AND A FEW MORE ...

I don't have space to include individual sections for every technique so I've summarised some more here. Beyond this, have a look for lists of fallacious arguments on the web. Just remember, most are not effective and, if you possibly can, you should use a properly reasoned argument.

■ **False dichotomy** – only give the reader two options, despite there being many more. *Comparing a complete package with nothing at all, despite there being options for only part of the package.*

■ **You're a Nazi if you disagree** – link the alternative to your view to something unpleasant. *"Enforced redundancies are akin*

to corporate euthanasia. We strongly oppose any such Final
Solution."

- **Naturalistic fallacy** – if it's natural it must be good. *"Belladonna and Nightshade smoothie – 100% natural ingredients!"*

- **Bribes and threats** – direct threats are not something you want to put in writing but veiled bribes and threats are used all the time in business. These appeal directly to the powerful greed and fear emotions. Not good for long-term relations though. *"Acecorp shares its experiences of sub-contractors with our partners and peers across the industry"* – subtext: keep us happy or you won't work again.

- **Perfect/imperfect solution** – if there is a rival solution or option, try to find weaknesses. If it is perfect, claim it is too perfect to be credible. If it's not, highlight those omissions.

- **Prove a negative** – you can't prove something doesn't exist. You can claim your argument must be true if no one can prove it isn't. Has been used for millennia by people to 'prove' the existence of God. *"You can't prove my company can't deliver, therefore, you must assume it can."*

- **Beg the question** – this means avoiding the question. By carefully wording your statement, you can prove something is true because it is true, thus avoiding the question 'why is it true?' *"Our integrity cannot be questioned, as only a company with the highest moral standards can grow as big as we are."* This example begs the question 'can a company with low moral standards grow big?' Essentially, we end up saying 'we must have high integrity because we're big, and we're big because we have high integrity'.

SUMMARY

Wherever possible, use a well-crafted argument backed up with sound data. However, as a last resort, you may be able to carefully apply one or more of the following:

- **Assume causality** – it's no coincidence, there's so much evidence, how else could you explain it?

- **It's common sense, stupid** – even though intuition is often wrong, make people believe you by claiming your argument is common sense.

- **It's common knowledge** – everyone knows this is true so you should believe it too.

- **Abuse statistics** – ignore the base rate, compare extremes, bias your selection and find patterns in randomness. These will all produce impressive but misleading statistics.

- **Widen or narrow definitions** – tweak the meaning of a term until it suits your needs.

- **Flattery** – most people have high opinions of themselves so make them feel special, especially if they make the decision you want.

- **And more …**

  - False dichotomy

  - You're a Nazi

  - Naturalistic fallacy

  - Bribes and threats

  - Perfect/imperfect solution

  - Prove a negative

  - Beg the question.

THE END

And that's it! Or rather it isn't. This book has merely scratched the surface of persuasive writing. More detail on all this content can be found on the web and in a range of books, so get reading.

In the Appendices, there's a summary of the rules, some alternatives to supersized words, some useful tools and a worked example of the seven-step concise writing process.

Finally, if you take away nothing else from this book, remember these two points:

Reader Response equals Result

and

If following a rule makes your writing less persuasive, break it.

Appendix 1 Summary of rules

Chapter 1: Persuasive Writing

Rule 1: include a call to action in your document

Chapter 2   Tools for Persuasive Writing

Rule 2: toy with people's emotions for your own ends

Rule 3: talk directly to the reader using You, We and I

Rule 4: tell your readers about the benefits to them, not just the features

Rule 5: tell stories to your readers

Chapter 3   Persuasion – Beyond Logic

Rule 6: the reader is always right

Chapter 5   Conciseness equals Clarity

Rule 7: cut out jargon your reader will not be familiar with

Rule 8: write how you would talk unless you have to be formal

Rule 9: only use words of three syllables or more if you cannot use a shorter alternative

Rule 10: don't write sentences that require you to take a breath in the middle

Rule 11: vary sentence length

Rule 12: include one main point per sentence

Rule 13: cut down on your adjectives and adverbs

Rule 14: keep 'the' and 'that' to a minimum

Rule 15: adjective before noun

Rule 16: cull any words that don't help persuade your reader

Rule 17: use examples and analogies to improve your readers' understanding

Chapter 6   Verbs Equal Vigour

Rule 18: favour the active voice wherever possible

Rule 19: minimise nominalised nouns

Chapter 7   Mistakes

Rule 20: DO NOT rely on grammar checkers in word processors

Rule 21: don't rely on word processor spell checkers

Rule 22: use punctuation sparingly and accurately

Rule 23: get someone else to proofread your work

Chapter 8   Planning and Structuring

Rule 24: make your main point accessible

Chapter 9   Layout, Fonts and Formatting

Rule 25: white space is your friend

Rule 26: fully justify only if you have around ten to twelve words per line. Otherwise, left justify

Rule 27: use lots of meaningful headings, at least two or three per A4 page

Appendix 2 Supersized words and their alternatives

Supersized	Alternatives
accede	agree
acquiesce	agree
advantageous	helpful, good
ascertain	find out
circumvent	avoid, go around
commence	start
concur	agree
consequently	thus, as a result
constitute	form
designate	assign
envisage	picture, imagine
facilitate	help
implement (as a verb)	use, do
leverage (as a verb)	exploit
liaise with	work with, talk to
paradigm	view, perspective
predominant	main
reiterate	restate, repeat
render	make
terminate	end
transpire	turn out
utilise	use

Appendix 3 Recommended reading

Here's a list of books worth taking a look at. Some are about writing, but some are simply books I've mentioned in the text that in some way inspired or stimulated this book. Happy reading!

Baggini, J. (2008), *The Duck that Won the Lottery* (Granta Books)

Camp, L. (2007), *Can I Change Your Mind?* (A & C Black Publishers Ltd)

Cutts, M. (2009), *Oxford Guide to Plain English* (Oxford University Press)

Goldacre, B. (2009), *Bad Science* (Harper Perennial)

Lehrer, J. (2010), *The Decisive Moment* (Canongate Books)

Sutherland, S. (2007), *Irrationality* (Pinter & Martin)

Taylor, N. (2008), *Brilliant Business Writing* (Prentice Hall)

Weiner, E.S.C. and Delahunty, A. (1994), *The Oxford Guide to English Usage* (BCA)

Appendix 4 Persuasive writing flowchart

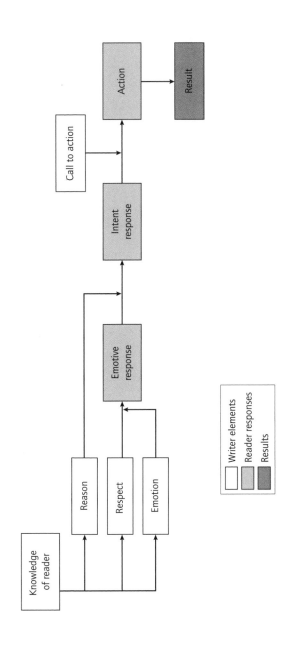

Appendix 5 Persuasive writing checklist

Reader:	Name (if known)	
	Gender	
	Age	
	Level of education	
	Occupation	
	Relationship to you	
	Reasons for reading	
	Where are they likely to read?	
	When are they are likely to read?	
	Cynicism rating	
Required Result		
Timescale to achieve result		
Reader action (what do you need them to do?)		
Emotive response (which emotions can you use and what reaction do you want?)		
Reputation (can you use yours/someone else's?)		
Reason (logically, why should they do what you ask?)		
Structure (which structure will you use?)		
Story/plot (will you tell a story and, if so, what is it?)		

Appendix 6 Exploiting and countering human decision-making

Chapter 3 presented many psychological techniques. This appendix gives you a handy reminder of how to exploit or counter their effects in your writing.

Primacy – people form opinions on first impressions and remember early information better.

> **Exploit**: summaries or abstracts; attention-grabbing headlines; go first if multiple views are presented.

> **Counter**: if someone else has got their view in first, use recency and put your point last.

Availability – information more easily recalled has more influence in decision-making.

> **Exploit**: shock the reader; relate your point to their personal experiences; tell stories: grab their attention though your document layout; use primacy and recency.

> **Counter**: present counter-anecdotes; confront the misconception (e.g. "I used to think this too but …"); cast doubt on the available evidence.

Consistency – once people have made up their mind, it is very difficult to change it. This is due to:

- sunk-cost bias – actual loss is more painful than potential loss;
- rationalisation – brain rewards you for twisting evidence to suit your existing views;
- confirmation bias – you only seek out evidence which agrees with your beliefs;
- social pressure – consistency is seen as strong.

Exploit: seek decisions from those who already agree; high-light investment so far; make confirmation points easy to find; praise the reader for consistency.

Counter: point out future savings; show how things have changed since opinion was formed (they didn't make a bad decision at the time); make confirmation hard to find; use analogies to show they would hold a different view in similar circumstances; show their social superiors agree with you.

Justification and evidence – people like to know why, even when the 'because' isn't that convincing; when deciding, it is easier to compare proportionately than exactly.

Exploit: explain why the reader should make a particular deci-sion; present comparisons proportionately wherever possible.

Counter: own up to a lack of evidence but appeal to their feelings and intuition (everyone loves to think they have good intuition so flatter them); show how any gamble has a very low cost; compare actual losses/gains if you are proportion-ately weaker.

Simplicity – people constantly seek the easy life and will con-vince themselves of a potential short cut's likely success.

Exploit: show how the decision you want makes their life easier. Find the decision-maker's particular pet hates and see if you can reduce them through your favoured decision. Offer additional benefits if needs be.

Counter: draw comparisons with other 'too good to be true' situations. Use examples and analogies to show success only comes from the long, hard route.

Loss and reward – we over-value what we have; if we make a quick decision we'll take the smaller, quicker reward; we aren't good at linking short-term gains with long-term cost; our brains do a crude subconscious cost/benefit analysis.

Exploit: offer short-term gains; emphasise what will be lost by making the wrong decision; make costs appear smaller than they are; show other attractive options to encourage the desire to choose something.

Counter: draw attention to long-term costs, avoid talking about costs/losses of your choice until subconscious decision is made.

Outside influences – people will look to others to help with the decision; people are most influenced by experience, conformity and aspiration.

Exploit: use references from people your reader will admire; create the appearance of expertise; show that everyone else is doing it.

Counter: encourage the reader to be an individual.

Repetition – find different ways to make the same point.

Anchoring – the brain will use nearby data for comparison if it doesn't have anything better.

Exploit: include consistently large or small numbers before your number to make it look better in comparison.

Counter: pay attention to the numbers surrounding your costs – eliminate numbers if necessary.

Halo/horns effect – if you are well-known for one good trait, you are assumed to be good in other traits and vice versa.

Exploit: use famous people as social proof; build a reputation for doing one thing brilliantly.

Counter: acknowledge your own reputation and show how things have changed; for rivals, use analogies to show how one good trait doesn't equal all-round competence.

Recency – the last thing read sticks in the mind; people are most likely to choose the last of three choices.

Exploit: give readers three choices with your favoured option at the end; write a concluding summary; try to get your opinion in last.

Counter: if you can't go last, go first; move unpleasant information to the middle or appendices.

Appendix 7 The seven-step concise writing process – worked example

Let's look at a real-world example from the first section of a grant for research funding. Note this was for a European programme with a high likelihood of a non-UK evaluator. This is important in terms of language choice. Whilst there is nothing fundamentally wrong with this extract, it does feel very long-winded and doesn't 'flow' as a story. Here's the original text:

Increased knowledge about consequences from water pollution and public desire for better quality water has prompted implementation of much stricter regulations by expanding scope of regulated contaminants and lowering their maximum contaminant levels (MCLs). Water resources available per each human being are diminishing as the population is rapidly growing. Reuse of industrial wastewaters and recovery of potential pollutants used in industrial processes becomes even more critical.

Although efforts to improve treatment of wastewater have resulted in a considerable improvement in the quality of fresh water and estuaries, industrial wastewater is still prevalent in Europe resulting in significant impact on different sectors of the economy and social life.

In many cases, the "quality" of the environment may be affected in ways such as negative impacts on aesthetics, foul odours, reduced fishing success and contamination of fish or shell-fish with direct negative impact to the eco-tourist and fishing industries. The resulting ecological and social impacts inevitably result in "knock-on" economic impacts, many of which are not addressed, e.g. financial costs incurred from the increased maintenance of rivers and waterways.

Water that is available for each human being on global level has fallen by 40% within the past 30 years. Europe is not spared this global shortage of water. ERA has highlighted: "One third of the European continent is under a threshold of 5,000 m³ per inhabitant per year – not only in the Mediterranean regions but also in certain densely populated and highly industrialised northern countries. At European level, 54% of water consumption is accounted for by industry, 26% by agriculture and 20% by domestic users, but this average breakdown may vary significantly from one country to another. The pressures exerted by increasing demand for water have led to over exploitation of local reserves in many regions. Moreover, 20 European countries are dependent for more than 10% of their supply on river water from neighbouring states and this figure rises to 75% in the case of the Netherlands and Luxembourg.

STEP 1: BULLETS

Plan your document using your favoured technique (see Chapter 8). Get to the point where you have a list of section headings. Complete each section in bullet-point form, with each bullet expressing only the most important points.

If you were writing from scratch, this is the point where you would draft out your major document points. Here, we have all the information so it is a case of picking them out. This section effectively says:

Regulation of water quality is increasing

Therefore industry needs to recycle waste water

Pollution has a big impact on water quality

There is very little available water in Europe

Most water is used by industry

STEP 2: STORY

Check your bullet points to make sure they tell an effective story. Is there a better order to make the points in? Have you missed a logical step?

Straight away, you can see this doesn't seem like a logical story flow. A 'Problem to Solution' structure would seem logical, as the project is looking to help companies recycle waste water. This gives the following structure:

Very little available water in Europe

Pollution is ruining what little is available

Regulation of water quality is increasing

Most water is used by industry

Therefore industry needs to recycle waste water

STEP 3: EXPAND

Draft out the document, adding as few words as possible to the bullet points to make complete sentences. The vast majority of added text should be supporting facts, not new parts to the story.

When reverse-engineering like this, it is simply a case of extracting the most useful facts that support your case and slotting them in with joining words. A first pass gives us:

The Water available for each human being on a global level has fallen by 40% within the past 30 years and, even in Europe, one third of the continent is under a threshold of 5,000 m³ per inhabitant p.a.

Water shortages are exacerbated by pollution from industrial wastewater, with impacts including aesthetics, foul odours, reduced fishing success and contamination of marine harvests, along with associated "knock-on" economic impacts.

Increased knowledge of water pollution consequences and public desire for better quality water has driven stricter regulations to lower maximum contaminant levels (MCLs). With 54% of water consumption accounted for by industry, reuse of industrial wastewaters becomes critical.

We've achieved a huge word-count reduction but it isn't yet polished. Next, we need to ensure each sentence isn't overloaded with too many points or unnecessary points.

STEP 4: CHECK THE SENTENCES

- **What does it actually say? Could this be misinterpreted?**
- **Do I need to say this? Does it add value?**
- **Are there other points made in the sentence that are not the main point? If so, can I remove them or move them into a separate sentence?**

The Water available for each human being on a global level has fallen by 40% within the past 30 years. Even in Europe, one third of the continent is under a threshold of 5,000 m³ per inhabitant p.a.

Water shortages are exacerbated by pollution from industrial wastewater. Impacts include aesthetics, foul odours, reduced fishing success and contamination of marine harvests, along with associated "knock-on" economic impacts.

Increased knowledge of water pollution consequences and public desire for better quality water has driven stricter regulations to lower maximum contaminant levels (MCLs). With 54% of water consumption accounted for by industry, reuse of industrial wastewaters becomes critical.

All we have done here is split the first two sentences. This takes the average words per sentence from 27 to 17, allowing the main points of the sentences to be taken in. All we need to do now is edit closely to make the section more punchy and readable

STEP 5: RE-READ THE SECTION AS A WHOLE

Do the sentences flow together? Has adding words modified the story?

Yep, happy enough so far.

STEP 6: CLOSE EDIT

Use some or all of the following techniques:

- **Summarise – can one word or phrase replace a list of similar items? Look out for the word 'and', as this is sometimes an indication of unnecessary additions.**

- **Eliminate unnecessary jargon – would an ignorant genius understand it?**

- **Edit for sentence length – try to keep the average sentence length under 20 words and provide lots of variation.**

If you have time:

- **Eliminate unnecessary adjectives/adverbs.**

■ **Remove 'the' and 'that' where possible.**

■ **Remove repetition – especially in multiple uses of the same description.**

Worldwide, water available per person has fallen 40% within the past 30 years. Even in Europe, one third of the continent has less than 5,000 m³ per person p.a.

Water shortages are made worse by pollution from industrial waste-water. Impacts include: aesthetics, foul odours, reduced fishing success and contamination of marine harvests, which in turn have "knock-on" economic consequences.

These impacts, coupled with a public desire for better quality water, have driven stricter regulations to lower maximum contaminant levels (MCLs). With 54% of water consumption accounted for by industry, reuse of industrial wastewater is critical.

Key points:

■ Simplified structure in the first sentence to reduce words and increase readability.

■ Replaced "under a threshold of" with "has less than" – plain English with greater clarity of meaning.

■ Replaced "exacerbated" with "made worse". I like the word 'exacerbated' but it is not in everyday use and may be difficult for someone with English as a second language.

■ Slightly re-worded the second paragraph for better logical flow, plus replaced "impacts" with "consequences" to reduce word repetition.

■ Removed "Increased knowledge of water pollution consequences" and replaced with "These impacts", as they effectively say the same thing. This also helps link the last two paragraphs together.

■ Replaced "becomes" with "is", as water reuse is already critical.

STEP 7: RE-READ AND PROOFREAD

Go away for a bit, come back and read straight through, out loud. Read in reverse and look for spelling/grammar errors.

Problems spotted in this document:

■ The 5,000m^3 statistic is meaningless as it has no benchmark to compare it with.

■ It would be nice to quantify the economic consequences.

■ The stricter regulations and the need to recycle aren't explicitly linked.

With these tweaks in place, the final text emerges:

Worldwide, water available per person has fallen 40% within the past 30 years. Even in Europe, one third of the continent has 'low' water resources (<5,000 m^3 per capita).

Water shortages are made worse by pollution from industrial wastewater. Impacts include: aesthetics, foul odours, reduced fishing success and contamination of marine harvests, costing billions of Euros each year.

These impacts, coupled with a public desire for better quality water, have driven stricter regulations to lower maximum contaminant levels (MCLs). With 54% of water consumption accounted for by industry, reuse of industrial wastewater is critical to meet these targets.

So what effect has all this editing had? Word count is down 70 per cent, sentence length is nearly halved (which aids readability) and all readability statistics are significantly improved. Most importantly, it is a more effective piece of text. There are still hundreds of changes you could make to this text but it is as important to know when to stop as it is to know how to start.

Exactly the same process applies if you are starting from scratch. Once you have worked out the points you want to make, follow the process and you will end up with tight, effective text. Remember, however, less is not always more if you lose persuasiveness.

Index